Jehovah's Witnesses

Jehovah's Witnesses

by

ANTHONY A. HOEKEMA

WILLIAM B. EERDMANS PUBLISHING COMPANY
Grand Rapids, Michigan

The material in this book is an updating of
material originally appearing in *The Four
Major Cults*, Fourth printing, August 1972.

Contents

Abbreviations

ASV	American Standard Version
KJ	King James Version
NWT	*New World Translation,* 1961 ed.
Paradise Lost	*From Paradise Lost to Paradise Regained*
Religion for Mankind	*What Has Religion Done for Mankind?*
RSV	Revised Standard Version
Survival After Death	*What Do the Scriptures Say about "Survival After Death"?*
You May Survive Armageddon	*You May Survive Armageddon into God's New World*
Your Will Be Done	*Your Will Be Done on Earth*

(Note: All Scripture quotations not otherwise identified are from the American Standard Version.)

Preface

The discussion of Jehovah's Witnesses found in this book is organized as follows: First, a brief history of the movement is given, in terms of the events that occurred during the presidencies of Charles Russell, Joseph Rutherford, and Nathan Knorr. Next comes a summary of statistics and activities. Then the question of the final source of authority for the group is taken up. The doctrines taught by Jehovah's Witnesses are next expounded in the order of the customary divisions of Christian theology: God, man, Christ, salvation, the church, the last things. An appendix critically examines Jehovah-Witness teaching on the person of Christ.

In setting forth the teachings of Jehovah's Witnesses, I have used primary sources exclusively (Watchtower Society publications). Whenever there was uncertainty about what was being taught on a certain doctrinal point, information was obtained directly from Watchtower leaders. References to the source materials used are given in the footnotes. A bibliography lists primary sources, Bible translations, histories of Jehovah's Witnesses, and a number of general works.

Readers of this book are referred to the author's *Four Major Cults* (Eerdmans, 1963) for further material. One will find in this last-named volume an appendix, not found in the present work, which deals critically with teachings common to both Jehovah's Witnesses and Seventh-day Adventists on "soul-extinction" in the intermediate state and on the final annihilation of the wicked. Besides setting forth the doctrinal teachings of Christian Science, Mormonism, and Seventh-day Adventism, *The Four Major Cults* also includes chapters on the challenge of the cults, the distinctive traits of the cult, and the approach to the cultist.

May the Lord use this book for the advancement of His kingdom and for the glory of His name. May He particularly use it to lead many from the errors of the Watchtower to the truth as it is in Christ.

Anthony A. Hoekema

Grand Rapids, Michigan
July, 1972

I. History

CHARLES TAZE RUSSELL

THE HISTORY OF JEHOVAH'S WITNESSES IS VERY CLOSELY TIED IN with the history of the three presidents of the organization who have so far held office. The first of these was Charles Taze Russell (1852-1916).[1] He was born in the town of Allegheny, now part of Pittsburgh, Pennsylvania, on February 16, 1852. His parents were Presbyterians of Scotch-Irish descent. At the age of fifteen Russell was already in partnership with his father, operating a chain of men's clothing stores. By this time he had joined the Congregational Church, finding it more to his liking than the Presbyterian.

Russell was soon troubled, however, by some of the doctrines taught in this church, the doctrines of predestination and eternal punishment giving him particular difficulty. By the time he was seventeen, in fact, he had become an avowed skeptic, discarding the Bible altogether. He explains how this happened in these words:

> Brought up a Presbyterian, indoctrinated from the Catechism, and being naturally of an inquiring mind, I fell a ready prey to the logic of infidelity, as soon as I began to think for myself. But that which at first threatened to be the utter shipwreck of faith in God and the Bible was, under God's providence, over-

[1] This biographical sketch is based chiefly on material found in two Watchtower publications: *Qualified to be Ministers* (Brooklyn, 1955), pp. 297-312; and *Jehovah's Witnesses in the Divine Purpose* (Brooklyn, 1959), pp. 14-63. Except where otherwise indicated, the information which follows has been gathered from the above-mentioned volumes.

ruled for good, and merely wrecked my confidence in human creeds and systems of Bible misinterpretations.[2]

One day in 1870 he dropped into a dusty, dingy basement hall near his Allegheny store

> to see if the handful who met there had anything more sensible to offer than the creeds of the great churches. There, for the first time, I heard something of the views of Second Adventism, by Jonas Wendell. . . .
>
> Though his Scripture exposition was not entirely clear, and though it was very far from what we now rejoice in, it was sufficient, under God, to re-establish my wavering faith in the Divine inspiration of the Bible. . . .[3]

His interest in Bible study aroused to fever pitch, Russell now organized a Bible class of six members who agreed to meet regularly. This group met in Pittsburgh from 1870-1875. Russell and his associates were disappointed by the Adventist view that Christ was coming again in the flesh, being convinced that His Second Coming would be a spiritual or invisible one. Russell therefore issued a pamphlet entitled *The Object and Manner of the Lord's Return,* of which some 50,000 copies were published.

In 1876 Russell came into contact with N. H. Barbour of Rochester, New York. Barbour was the leader of a group of disaffected Adventists who had left that movement because they, like Russell, believed that the Second Coming of Christ was to be a spiritual, non-visible one. The Pittsburgh group and the Rochester group now joined, with the result that the magazine *The Herald of the Morning,* formerly published by Barbour, became a joint venture. In 1877 Barbour and Russell jointly published a 194-page book entitled *Three Worlds or Plan of Redemption.*

---

[2] *Watchtower* magazine, 1916, pp. 170-71; quoted in *Jehovah's Witnesses in the Divine Purpose,* p. 14. Note here a typical cult phenomenon: the rejection of all "human creeds."

[3] *Jehovah's Witnesses in the Divine Purpose,* p. 14. It is important to note that, by his own admission, it was the Adventists who delivered Russell from his early skepticism. Though the term "Second Adventism" which is used in the quotation does not represent any known Adventist denomination, I conclude, from the similarities which exist between Seventh-day Adventist doctrines and Jehovah-Witness teachings, that this group was either a Seventh-day Adventist congregation, or a group of Adventists who held doctrines similar to those of Seventh-day Adventism. From the Adventists Russell obviously borrowed such doctrines as the extinction of the soul at death, the annihilation of the wicked, the denial of hell, and a modified form of the investigative judgment.

This book set forth their belief that Christ's second presence began invisibly in the fall of 1874 and thereby commenced a forty-year harvest period. Then, remarkably accurately, they set forth the year 1914 as the end of the Gentile times. . . .[4]

In a few years, however, Russell broke with Barbour because the latter began to deny that the death of Christ was the ransom price for Adam and his race. Russell now started a new periodical called *Zion's Watch Tower and Herald of Christ's Presence,* the first issue coming off the press on July 1, 1879.[5]

The new magazine proved to be an important factor in the expansion of the movement. By 1880, for example, some thirty congregations had come into existence in seven states. Zion's Watch Tower Tract Society was established as an unincorporated body in 1881, with Russell as its manager. On December 13, 1884, this Society was granted a legal charter and was organized as a corporation; we may therefore recognize this date as the official beginning of the Jehovah's Witness movement.[6] The purpose of the society, as stated in Article II of the charter, was "the dissemination of Bible truths in various languages by means of the publication of tracts, pamphlets, papers and other religious documents, and by the use of all other lawful means. . . ."[7]

In accordance with this purpose Russell now issued the first of what was eventually to become a 7-volume series of doctrinal books. This first volume, appearing in 1886, was called *The Divine Plan of the Ages.* The entire series, first called *Millennial Dawn,* later came to be called *Studies in the Scriptures.* These books had a wide circulation; over six million copies of the first volume were distributed.

In 1889 the society acquired a building in Allegheny, Pennsylvania, which served as its headquarters for the next twenty years.

---

[4] *Qualified to be Ministers,* p. 300. It will be noted, therefore, that as early as 1877 Russell specified that Christ had invisibly returned in 1874.

[5] Though at first this magazine was published monthly, in 1892 it began to appear semi-monthly. In 1909 its name was changed to *The Watch Tower and Herald of Christ's Presence;* in 1939 the name became *The Watchtower and Herald of Christ's Kingdom;* later in that same year the title by which it still appears was assumed: *The Watchtower Announcing Jehovah's Kingdom (Jehovah's Witnesses in the Divine Purpose,* p. 21, note m).

[6] Though at first the society went by the above-mentioned name, in 1896 the name was changed to Watch Tower Bible and Tract Society of Pennsylvania (*Qualified to be Ministers,* p. 303).

[7] *Ibid.,* p. 304.

Russell made his first trip abroad in 1891, and in 1900 the society's first branch office was established in London. Soon books and pamphlets began to be published in languages other than English. In 1903, while Russell was on a second European tour, a branch of the society was set up in Germany; in 1904 one was opened in Australia.

A new avenue of expansion opened up when, in 1908, Joseph Franklin Rutherford, the society's legal counselor, obtained property for the society in Brooklyn, New York. In order to hold this property, the society had to form another corporation; hence in 1909 the People's Pulpit Association of New York was incorporated.[8]

In *Jehovah's Witnesses in the Divine Purpose* it is said that during the years 1909-1914 Russell's sermons were sent out weekly to about 3,000 newspapers in the United States, Canada, and Europe (p. 50). Martin and Klann, however, in their *Jehovah of the Watchtower,* give documentary evidence to prove that in many cases these sermons were never delivered, as reported, in the places claimed. From the *Brooklyn Daily Eagle* of February 19, 1912, the authors quote a news story affirming that a sermon allegedly delivered by Russell in Honolulu on a certain date was never preached.[9] On a later page the authors reproduce a photostatic copy of a letter sent to the *Brooklyn Daily Eagle* by a Honolulu editor stating that on the designated day Russell had stopped in Honolulu for a few hours, but had made no public address.[10]

Martin and Klann also tell how Russell's periodical once advertised so-called "Miracle Wheat" for one dollar a pound, claiming that it would grow five times as fast as any other brand. After the *Brooklyn Daily Eagle* had published a cartoon ridiculing the "Pastor" and his "miracle wheat," Russell sued the newspaper for libel. When this wheat was investigated by government depart-

---

[8] In 1956 the name of this corporation was changed to the one it now bears: Watchtower Bible and Tract Society of New York, Inc. There is also a British corporation, which was formed in 1914, under the name International Bible Students Association; it has a Brooklyn address as well as a London address. The work of the organization is done by all three of these corporations; it is the Pennsylvania corporation, however, which is the controlling body and which provides the other corporations with financial support (*Jehovah's Witnesses in the Divine Purpose,* pp. 48-49).

[9] Walter R. Martin and Norman H. Klann, *Jehovah of the Watchtower,* rev. ed. (Grand Rapids: Zondervan, 1959), pp. 15-17.

[10] *Ibid.,* opposite p. 30.

ments, however, it was found to be, not five times as good as, but slightly inferior to, ordinary wheat. Needless to say, the *Eagle* won the suit.[11]

It should be mentioned at this point that Russell was married in 1879 to Maria Frances Ackley. No children were born of this union. For many years Mrs. Russell was active in the Watchtower Society, serving as the first secretary-treasurer of the society and for many years as associate editor of the *Watch Tower*. In 1897, however, she and Russell separated. In 1913 Mrs. Russell sued her husband for divorce on the grounds of "his conceit, egotism, domination, and improper conduct in relation to other women."[12]

Russell's appalling egotism is evident from a comment made by him about his *Scripture Studies* series:

> . . . Not only do we find that people cannot see the divine plan in studying the Bible by itself, but we see, also, that if anyone lays the "Scripture Studies" aside, even after he has used them, after he has become familiar with them, after he has read them for ten years — if he then lays them aside and ignores them and goes to the Bible alone, though he has understood his Bible for ten years, our experience shows that within two years he goes into darkness. On the other hand, if he had merely read the "Scripture Studies" with their references and had not read a page of the Bible as such, he would be in the light at the end of two years, because he would have the light of the Scriptures.[13]

Russell, in other words, considered his books so indispensable for the proper understanding of Scripture that without them one would simply remain in spiritual darkness.

In June, 1912, the Rev. Mr. J. J. Ross, pastor of the James Street Baptist Church of Hamilton, Ontario, published a denunciatory pamphlet about Russell entitled *Some Facts about the Self-*

---

11 *Ibid.*, p. 14. The authors quote from the Nov. 1, 1916, issue of the *Daily Eagle,* which contained an obituary article about Russell.

12 Bruce M. Metzger, "The Jehovah's Witnesses and Jesus Christ," *Theology Today,* April, 1953, pp. 65-66. Dr. Metzger refers his readers to Herbert H. Stroup's *The Jehovah's Witnesses* (New York: Columbia University Press, 1945), pp. 9-11, for a more detailed account of the divorce proceedings.

13 *Watch Tower,* Sept. 15, 1910, p. 298; quoted in Martin and Klann, *op. cit.,* p. 24. See also J. K. Van Baalen's *Chaos of Cults,* 3rd ed., p. 269, n. 2, where this same passage is quoted from the July, 1957, *Watchtower.*

styled "Pastor," Charles T. Russell.[14] Russell sued Ross for libel. In the trial, which took place the following year, Russell was proved to be a perjurer. When asked by Attorney Staunton, Ross's lawyer, whether he knew the Greek alphabet, Russell replied, "Oh, yes." When he was further asked to identify the Greek letters on top of a page of the Greek Testament which was handed him, he was unable to do so, finally admitting that he was not familiar with the Greek language.[15] Russell, furthermore, had previously claimed to have been ordained by a recognized religious body. Staunton also pressed him on this point, finally asking him point-blank, "Now, you never were ordained by a bishop, clergyman, presbytery, council, or any body of men living?" Russell answered, after a long pause, "I never was."[16] In this trial, therefore, Russell's deliberate perjury was established beyond doubt, and the real character of the man looked up to by his followers as an inspired religious teacher was clearly revealed.

Russell died on October 31, 1916, while aboard a train near Pampa, Texas, on his way home from a California speaking trip. It is claimed by Jehovah's Witnesses that during his lifetime he traveled more than a million miles, gave more than 30,000 sermons, and wrote books totalling over 50,000 pages.[17]

JOSEPH FRANKLIN RUTHERFORD

On January 6, 1917, Joseph Franklin Rutherford, who had been serving as the society's legal counselor, became the second president of the Watchtower Society.[18] Rutherford was born on November 8, 1869, in Booneville, Missouri, of Baptist parents. When he was sixteen years old, he entered college for the purpose of studying law. At the age of twenty-two he was admitted to the bar and began to practice law, later serving four years as public prosecutor for Booneville. Still later he was appointed special judge for the Fourteenth Judicial District of Missouri. During

---

[14] Martin and Klann, *op. cit.*, p. 18.

[15] *Ibid.*, p. 20. The authors quote from a copy of the Russell-vs.-Ross transcript on file in the Brooklyn headquarters of the Watchtower Society.

[16] *Ibid.*, p. 22. For the entire story of this trial, which includes other examples of Russell's deliberate lying under oath, the reader is referred to pp. 18-22 of Martin and Klann.

[17] *Qualified to be Ministers*, p. 310.

[18] This sketch of the history of the Jehovah's Witnesses during Rutherford's presidency is based chiefly on pp. 312-32 of *Qualified to be Ministers*, and on pp. 64-195 of *Jehovah's Witnesses in the Divine Purpose*.

this time he occasionally served as substitute judge when the regular judge was ill. Hence he came to be called "Judge" Rutherford. In 1894 Rutherford came into contact with representatives of the Watchtower Society; in 1906 he joined the movement; and in 1907 he became the society's legal counselor.

When he became president, Rutherford proceeded at once to reorganize the Brooklyn office and to encourage the members of the society to engage in a more active program of witnessing. Shortly after Rutherford's accession to the presidency, dissatisfaction arose within the ranks of the society. This dissatisfaction culminated in open rebellion, after which the leaders of the disaffected group were dismissed from their official positions. This dismissal led to the formation of certain schismatic groups.

In July of 1917 the seventh volume of the *Studies in the Scriptures* series, *The Finished Mystery*, was published. This book, which was compiled by Watchtower editors from the writings of Charles T. Russell, was chiefly a commentary on Revelation and Ezekiel. A 4-page extract from this book entitled "The Fall of Babylon" was distributed in great quantities to church members, beginning on December 30, 1917. According to this tract, Catholic and Protestant religious organizations together form present-day Babylon which, it was predicted, would soon pass into oblivion. The furor which the tract aroused soon led to governmental action. In February of 1918 the Canadian government forbade anyone to possess copies of Watchtower publications; it was alleged that they contained seditious and anti-war statements.[19] William J. Schnell, a former Jehovah's Witness who left the movement, asserts that during this time Rutherford was pursuing "a seemingly anti-war editorial policy" in the *Watchtower* magazine.[20] In May of 1918 warrants were issued by the United States District Court of Eastern New York for the arrest of eight of the society's leaders, including Rutherford, charging them with conspiring to cause insubordination and refusal of duty in United States military and naval forces.[21] On June 20 the eight were found guilty of these charges, and the next day they were sentenced to twenty years imprisonment in the federal penitentiary at Atlanta, Georgia.[22]

19 *Jehovah's Witnesses in the Divine Purpose*, pp. 75-76.
20 *Thirty Years a Watch Tower Slave* (Grand Rapids: Baker, 1956), p. 37.
21 *Qualified to be Ministers*, p. 315.
22 *Ibid.* Actually, to eighty years, since they were sentenced to twenty years each on four different counts (*Jehovah's Witnesses in the Divine Purpose*, p. 80).

The Brooklyn headquarters were now closed, operations of the society being conducted, for the time being, from Pittsburgh. After the war ended in November of 1918, society members began to petition their congressmen and governors for the release of the Watchtower leaders. On May 14, 1919, the convictions of the eight leaders were reversed, and soon thereafter they were set free.[23]

The Brooklyn office was now reopened, and the society received a new lease on life. During the course of this year a second magazine, *The Golden Age,* was launched, the first issue appearing on October 1, 1919.[24]

Printing activities were now expanded, the society deciding to do all its own printing. In 1921 the society published *The Harp of God,* the first of a series of books by Rutherford, who proved to be an even more prolific writer than Russell had been.[25] Soon the Rutherford books were replacing Russell's volumes as standard expositions of Watchtower doctrine.

In 1920 all the members of the congregations who participated in the witnessing work of the society were required to turn in weekly reports. William J. Schnell, whose *Thirty Years a Watch Tower Slave* is a revealing account of the inner workings of the movement, contends that during Rutherford's presidency there emerged a basic change in Watchtower policies. Whereas emphasis had previously been laid on Bible study, character development, and the cultivation of the fruits of the Spirit, all the stress came to be laid on the placing of literature, the making of calls, and the reporting of these calls to Watchtower Headquarters. Schnell claims that as a result of this change of purpose, more than three-fourths of the Bible Students originally associated with the movement left the group.[26]

In connection with the increased emphasis on witnessing, there began to appear, in October of 1922, a monthly service sheet of instructions called *The Bulletin.* Though these instructions had been issued since 1917 to "pioneers," who devoted full time to witnessing, they were now made available to all members of the society to help them in their propagandizing activities.[27]

[23] *Qualified to be Ministers,* p. 316.
[24] The name of this semi-monthly was changed in 1937 to *Consolation;* in 1946 the name was changed to *Awake,* under which title it is still published (*Jehovah's Witnesses in the Divine Purpose,* p. 89, note v).
[25] See the bibliography for Rutherford's other publications.
[26] *Op. cit.,* pp. 29, 41, 42.
[27] In 1935 the name of this monthly was changed to *Director;* in 1936, to *Informant;* and in 1956, to *Kingdom Ministry* (*Jehovah's Wit-*

In 1931, at a convention held at Columbus, Ohio, the members of the society adopted a resolution affirming that, from then on, they were to be known as *Jehovah's Witnesses,* basing this new name particularly on the words of Isaiah 43:10, "Ye are my witnesses, saith Jehovah, and my servant whom I have chosen. . . ."[28]

In 1940 the society began its street distribution of the *Watchtower* and *Consolation* magazines, offering them to people on street corners. This policy is still followed. Another witnessing method which had been in vogue from 1934 — the playing of phonograph records at the doors of homes — was abandoned in 1944, however, in favor of personal presentations by the members.[29]

During World War II the policy of neutrality which the society had adopted in 1917 was reaffirmed, with the result that many Jehovah's Witnesses were convicted and imprisoned for refusing to serve in the armed forces. After 1940 most male witnesses were able to establish their ministerial status before their local draft boards so as to obtain 4-D exemptions from military service. Not all were successful in obtaining such exemptions, however; hence some 3,500 Witnesses were imprisoned during the war years.[30] It is significant to note that the number of Jehovah-Witness "ministers" doubled between the years 1939 and 1945, the number given for the latter year being 141,606.[31]

On January 8, 1942, Rutherford died. He had been president of the society for twenty-five years. During his presidency the society moved from a more or less democratic organization to a "theocratic" one,[32] in which the directors of the various local con-

---

nesses in the Divine Purpose, p. 104 and p. 148, n. u).

28 *Jehovah's Witnesses in the Divine Purpose,* pp. 125-126. The entire text of the resolution is there reproduced.

29 *Qualified to be Ministers,* p. 334.

30 *Ibid.,* pp. 327-31. The statement about "most male witnesses" is found on p. 331. On pp. 223-24 of *Jehovah's Witnesses in the Divine Purpose,* however, we are told that, during these war years, only a few Jehovah's Witnesses were given ministerial exemption. One wonders how these two apparently contradictory statements can be reconciled.

31 *Qualified to be Ministers,* p. 332. "Ministers" are Jehovah's Witnesses who are actively engaged in witnessing. Even those who do not devote their full time to these religious activities are considered by the group to be "ministers."

32 "Theocratic" means *God-ruled.* Since Jehovah's Witnesses believe that they are directly ruled by God, the adjective "theocratic" is applied by them not only to their type of organization, but also to all their activities: they speak of "theocratic ministry," "theocratic warfare," and so on.

gregations were no longer elected by local assemblies, but were appointed by the governing body in Brooklyn.[33]

NATHAN HOMER KNORR

On January 13, 1942, Nathan H. Knorr was elected to be the society's third president.[34]   He was born in 1905 in Bethlehem, Pennsylvania. At the age of sixteen he had already resigned his membership in the Reformed Church and had associated himself with the Allentown, Pennsylvania, congregation of Jehovah's Witnesses. At the age of eighteen he became a full-time preacher, and joined the headquarters staff in Brooklyn. Soon he was made co-ordinator of all printing activities in the society plant, becoming general manager of the publishing office and plant in 1932.   In 1934 he became one of the directors of the New York corporation, and in 1940 he became vice-president of the Pennsylvania corporation.[35]

Knorr is not as well known as the previous two society presidents were; few outsiders even know his name. One of his major concerns while in office has been the improvement of the society's training program. A major step in this new educational program was the establishment, in 1943, of the Gilead Watchtower Bible School in South Lansing, New York (near Ithaca). An important next step was the organization of "theocratic ministry schools" in every Jehovah's Witness congregation. In order to aid the congregations in their local training programs, three text-books, containing information about Bible contents, witnessing methods, and history, were published over a ten-year period: *Theocratic Aid to Kingdom Publishers* (1945), *Equipped for Every Good Work* (1946), and *Qualified to be Ministers* (1955).

In addition to the above titles, a new series of doctrinal books is being published during Knorr's presidency. Unlike previous Watchtower publications, however, these books are not the work of a single author. Although it is surmised that Mr. Knorr is their primary author, the books pass through several hands before publication,[36] and are issued anonymously. One of the first of these

[33] *Qualified to be Ministers,* p. 320.
[34] The following information about the history of the Jehovah's Witnesses since 1942 is based chiefly on pp. 332-45 of *Qualified to be Ministers,* and on pp. 196-295 of *Jehovah's Witnesses in the Divine Purpose.*
[35] *Jehovah's Witnesses in the Divine Purpose,* p. 196.
[36] This information was obtained from Mr. Ulysses V. Glass, Press Secretary to Mr. Knorr, in an interview at Brooklyn Headquarters on June 6, 1962.

books, which are now considered authoritative doctrinal guides by the Witnesses, taking the place of previous publications by Russell and Rutherford, was *The Truth Shall Make You Free,* published in 1943. In 1946 came *Let God Be True,* a Jehovah-Witness doctrinal summary, which was revised in 1952, and of which, so it is claimed, more than 17,000,000 copies have been printed, in 50 languages. *Make Sure of All Things,* which first appeared in 1953 and was revised in 1957, is a compilation of Scripture passages on seventy topics; Jehovah's Witnesses use this volume as a handy Scripture reference book when making calls. *From Paradise Lost to Paradise Regained,* published in 1958, represents a new format: the type is larger and easier to read than that used in the other books, and there are many illustrations. By means of these publications, which have been sold by the millions, the society now spreads its teachings far and wide.[37]

Another important project carried out during Knorr's presidency has been the translation of the Bible into modern English. In 1950 the first of these translations appeared: *The New World Translation of the Christian Greek Scriptures.* The translation of the Old Testament has been released in portions: Volume I was published in 1953, Volume II in 1955, Volume III in 1957, Volume IV in 1958, and Volume V in 1960. In 1961 the entire Bible in the *New World Translation* was published in one volume. The translators make clear that this one-volume edition may be considered a revised edition of the *New World Translation,* since certain changes from previous editions have been made in it.[38] The names of the members of the New World Bible Translation Committee which did the translating are not divulged; the members of this committee have requested that they remain anonymous even after their death.[39] This translation is by no means an objective rendering of the Bible into English; it incorporates many features which support Jehovah-Witness doctrines.[40]

During Knorr's regime as president, there has been a tremendous expansion of the work into foreign countries. Whereas in 1942

[37] For other titles published since Knorr assumed the presidency, see the bibliography.
[38] *New World Translation of the Holy Scriptures,* revised A.D. 1961 (Watchtower Society, 1961), p. 6.
[39] *Jehovah's Witnesses in the Divine Purpose,* p. 258.
[40] For scholarly and competent analyses of these translations, the reader is referred to Bruce M. Metzger, *op. cit.,* pp. 67, 74-80; and to Walter E. Stuermann, "Jehovah's Witnesses," *Interpretation,* Vol. V, No. 3 (July, 1956), pp. 323-45. See below, pp. 26-30.

witnessing was carried on in only 54 countries, in 1971 work was done in 207 countries.[41]

Among the most publicized aspects of Jehovah-Witness activity during the fifties were the Yankee Stadium conventions in New York City, which were attended by Witnesses from all over the world. The Yankee Stadium Assembly held in 1950 attracted a peak attendance of 123,707;[42] the 1953 assembly reported a top attendance of 165,829;[43] and the 1958 assembly, held simultaneously in Yankee Stadium and the Polo Grounds, drew a record attendance on Sunday, August 3, of 253,922 persons.[44]

STATISTICS AND ACTIVITIES

Though the Watchtower Society keeps no membership roll, it does keep a record of the preaching activities of Jehovah's Witnesses. Since 1948, the January 1 issue of *The Watchtower* has contained the so-called "Service Year Report" for the preceding year. From the January 1, 1972, issue we glean the following information: in 1971 the average number of active Jehovah's Witnesses throughout the world was 1,510,245.[45] This figure represents an increase over the previous service year of 125,000.[46]

Jehovah's Witnesses do not recognize ordination in the sense in which Christian churches do; every active Witness is called a "minister." The closest analogy to an ordained minister among the Jehovah's Witnesses is a "pioneer publisher" — a person who devotes his full time to witnessing and distributing literature. In 1971 the average number of pioneer publishers throughout the world was

[41] *Qualified to be Ministers*, p. 340; *Watchtower*, Jan. 1, 1972, p. 25.
[42] *Qualified to be Ministers*, p. 342.
[43] *Ibid.*, p. 344.
[44] *Jehovah's Witnesses in the Divine Purpose*, p. 291.
[45] *Watchtower*, Jan. 1, 1972, p. 25. This is the figure given for "1971 Av. Pubs." Pubs. stands for publishers, a common designation for active Witnesses. Since it is said on p. 27 of this issue that these individuals "arranged to go from house to house or to declare the good news of God's kingdom in some other way every month during the past year," we may assume that this figure represents the total number of regularly active Witnesses for the year. Because the Jehovah-Witness service year runs from Oct. 1 to Oct. 1, this figure reflects the situation as of Sept. 30, 1971. The article from which the above figure was taken goes on to say, "However, before the year ended, the number [of publishers] grew to 1,590,793" (p. 27). Apparently the number of adherents far exceeds the number of active Witnesses, since the number who attended the Memorial or Lord's Supper in 1971 is given as 3,453,542 (p. 25).
[46] *Ibid.*, p. 27. The report also states that 149,808 people were baptized in 1971.

95,501. The total number of congregations listed for the year 1971 was 27,154.[47]

What is the geographical distribution of Jehovah's Witnesses? The average number of active Witnesses in the United States for 1971 was 402,893.[48] This figure represents twenty-seven percent of the average number of active Witnesses in the world during that year. In 1971, therefore, the relationship of active Witnesses in the United States to those outside the United States was as follows: twenty-seven percent in the United States, and seveny-three percent in foreign countries. In other words, in 1971 approximately three out of every four active Jehovah's Witnesses were to be found outside the United States.

From the January 1, 1972, issue of *The Watchtower* we learn, further, that the foreign country in which the most Jehovah's Witnesses were found in 1971 is West Germany (87,976 active Witnesses listed). Next is Nigeria, with 75,372; then Brazil, with 66,460. The British Isles come next with 62,813; then the Philippines, with 54,264; and then Zambia, with 52,369. 51,256 active Witnesses are listed for Mexico, and 48,100 for Canada. Other countries where the Witnesses claim to have had at least 5,000 active workers in 1971 include Argentina, Australia, Austria, Belgium, Chile, Colombia, Congo (Kinshasa), Denmark, Finland, France, Ghana, Greece, Italy, Jamaica, Japan, Korea, New Zealand, Norway, Portugal, Puerto Rico, Rhodesia, Malawi, South Africa, Spain, Sweden, Switzerland, and Venezuela.[49]

During the year 1971 Jehovah's Witnesses claim to have put in 291,952,375 hours of witnessing, and to have distributed 18,168,-032 bound books and Bibles, 10,590,176 booklets, and 213,898,563 copies of *The Watchtower* and *Awake*. It is further stated that they made 133,785 back calls and conducted 1,257,904 Bible studies in 1971.[50]

As was noted previously, the two chief Jehovah-Witness periodicals are *The Watchtower* and *Awake*, each of which appears bi-

[47] Both of the above figures were obtained from the Jan. 1, 1972, *Watchtower*, p. 25.

[48] *Ibid.*, p. 22. It is interesting to note, however, that separate figures are given for Alaska (823) and Hawaii (3,450).

[49] A great many more countries are listed where a smaller number of active workers are found. It must be remembered, of course, that I am simply reproducing Jehovah-Witness figures here. We are not told how these figures are arrived at, nor what criterion is used to determine whether a person is a publisher (active worker).

[50] *Watchtower*, Jan. 1, 1972, pp. 25, 27.

weekly, one alternating with the other. In the July 15, 1972, issue of *The Watchtower* it is claimed that 7,850,000 copies of this issue were printed, in 74 languages. The July 8, 1972, issue of *Awake* reports an average printing of 7,500,000 copies, in 27 languages.

Most of the literature of the society is printed and bound at its own printing plant in Brooklyn, New York. Some idea of the scope of this work may be gained from the fact that of one of the society's books, *The Truth that Leads to Eternal Life*, published in 1968, 53 million copies have been printed in 76 languages.[51] All those working at the printing plant receive room and board, a modest yearly clothing allowance, and fourteen dollars a month.[52] This extremely low salary is undoubtedly one of the biggest reasons why Jehovah's Witnesses can still sell most of their bound books for as little as fifty cents a copy.

Office workers at Bethel Headquarters (as the Brooklyn apartment and office building is called) work for the same "salary" as the employees of the printing plant. In addition, there are two "Kingdom farms" — one near Ithaca, New York, and one about fifty miles from New York City — which provide vegetables, fruit, and dairy products for the "Bethel family."

For approximately thirty years the Watchtower Society owned and operated Radio Station WBBR on Staten Island, New York. In 1937, however, the society withdrew from the commercial use of radio, and in 1957 Radio Station WBBR was sold.[53]

As far as is known, the society operates no hospitals, sanatoriums, clinics, or dispensaries. There are no Jehovah-Witness elementary schools, high schools, or colleges. It has been noted, however, that in 1943 the Gilead Bible School was opened. In 1960 this school was moved from its former location in South Lansing, New York, to 107 Columbia Heights in Brooklyn — across the street from Bethel Headquarters.[54] This school has facilities for about 100 students; it has a twenty-week curriculum, divided into four quarters of five weeks each.[55] The students, many of whom come from foreign countries, are trained in such subjects as Bible content, doctrines, languages of the countries in which they will be working, and minis-

---

[51] Letter from the Watchtower Bible and Tract Society dated July 4, 1972.
[52] *Ibid.* It should be remembered, however, that the people thus housed are either single individuals or married couples without children. There are no facilities at Bethel Headquarters in Brooklyn for married couples with children.
[53] *Jehovah's Witnesses in the Divine Purpose*, pp. 120, 138, 283.
[54] 1961 *Yearbook of Jehovah's Witnesses*, p. 59.
[55] Watchtower brochure entitled *Watchtower Bible School of Gilead*, p. 2.

terial activities.[56] There are other training schools in foreign countries, which give instruction on the Bible-school level for the various types of Jehovah-Witness ministry.[57]

As far as the organization of the Watchtower Society is concerned, mention has already been made of the three corporations under which the society operates, and of its "theocratic" method of appointing people to positions of leadership. Below the central controlling powers are the so-called "regional servants," of which there are six in the United States. These supervise the work done in their areas, and report to the Board of Directors. Under these are the "zone servants," which number 153 in the United States. These must work with the congregations in their zones and must conduct occasional "zone assemblies" at which the constituent groups meet together.[58] The local groups, which are never larger than two hundred, are called "companies" or "congregations," and the person in charge of each congregation is called a "company servant."[59] The congregations meet in unpretentious buildings called "Kingdom Halls."[60]

Though Jehovah's Witnesses do not actually prohibit smoking, the practice is frowned upon. It is said that smoking pollutes the body and should therefore be avoided. There is no specific ban on drinking alcoholic beverages, but anyone drinking to excess will be disfellowshiped.[61]

Jehovah's Witnesses consider Christmas to be "a celebration that is neither commanded nor mentioned in Scripture, but that was borrowed from . . . pagan celebrations"[62]; they oppose the use of Christmas trees.[63] They are unalterably opposed to blood transfusions,[64] and they refuse to salute the flag of any nation.[65] Though they do pay taxes and make social security payments, they do not vote or hold political office.[66] In times of war Jehovah's Witnesses take a position of strict neutrality. They claim

[56] *Ibid.*, pp. 2-3.
[57] *Jehovah's Witnesses in the Divine Purpose*, p. 293.
[58] *Ibid.*, pp. 189-90.
[59] *Ibid.*, p. 189.
[60] For most of the above information I am indebted to Charles S. Braden, *These Also Believe*, pp. 365-66.
[61] Letter to the author from Watchtower Headquarters dated Jan. 21, 1963.
[62] *Awake*, Dec. 8, 1961, p. 8.
[63] Braden, *These Also Believe*, p. 379.
[64] *Make Sure of All Things*, p. 47.
[65] *Let God Be True*, 2nd ed. (1952), pp. 242-43.
[66] Personal interview with Ulysses V. Glass, June 6, 1962.

that "the preaching activity of Jehovah's ministers entitles them to claim exemption from performing military training and service in the armed forces," adding that they have conscientious objections to noncombatant as well as to combatant military service.[67]

There have been a number of defections from the Jehovah-Witness movement. One of the best known is the so-called *Dawn Bible Students' Association,* which broke away from the parent group after Russell's death; its headquarters are in East Rutherford, New Jersey. Another prominent splinter group is the so-called *Laymen's Home Missionary Movement,* which originated in 1917. The first leader of this group was Paul S. L. Johnson; its headquarters are in Philadelphia. Kurt Hutten is of the opinion that approximately twenty groups have left the Jehovah's Witnesses.[68]

[67] Letter from Watchtower Headquarters, Jan. 21, 1963.
[68] *Die Glaubenswelt des Sektierers* (Hamburg: Furche-Verlag, 1957) p. 96.

II. Source of Authority

NORM FOR INTERPRETING SCRIPTURE

As we begin our examination of the doctrinal teachings of Jehovah's Witnesses, we shall first of all take up the question of their source of authority. The Watchtower Society has not issued a set of statements of belief comparable to the "Fundamental Beliefs of Seventh-day Adventists," or the "Articles of Faith" of the Mormons. To find the teachings of Jehovah's Witnesses on various doctrinal points we must consult their publications. It will be recalled that the anonymous books and booklets published since 1942 are now considered their authoritative doctrinal guides, replacing earlier publications authored by Russell and Rutherford.

When we approach these publications with the question, What do Jehovah's Witnesses consider to be their ultimate source of authority? the answer seems to be the same as that given by the Protestant churches: namely, the Bible. "The Holy Scriptures of the Bible are the standard by which to judge all religions."[69] Scripture, it is said, is the written revelation of the true God[70]; the Bible is therefore not a human product, but a book of which God is the primary author and inspirer.[71]

In *Let God Be True,* a widely circulated and well-known Jehovah-Witness doctrinal book, it is unequivocally stated, "We shall let God be found true by turning our readers to his imperishable written Word."[72] On another page it is said,

[69] *What Has Religion Done for Mankind?* (Brooklyn: Watchtower Bible and Tract Society, 1951), p. 32.
[70] *Ibid.,* p. 26.
[71] *Ibid.,* pp. 29-31.
[72] Rev. ed. (Brooklyn, 1952), p. 18.

> To let God be found true means to let God have the say as
> to what is the truth that sets men free. It means to accept his
> Word, the Bible, as the truth.   Hence, in this book, our appeal
> is to the Bible for truth.   Our obligation is to back up what
> is said herein by quotations from the Bible for proof of truth-
> fulness and reliability.[73]

And another statement appears later in the volume: "The Word
of the Most High God is the dependable basis for faith."[74]   From
both Old Testament and New Testament it is shown that the oral
traditions of men were not considered authoritative either by the
Bible writers or by Jesus Christ; hence the authors of *Let God Be
True* decisively reject such a second source of authority next to
the Bible.[75]

We gratefully recognize that Jehovah's Witnesses thus clearly
state their dependence on Scripture as their final source of authority.   As we examine their theology, however, it will become
quite evident that this is by no means a fair and honest statement
of the case.   Instead of listening to Scripture and subjecting themselves wholly to its teachings, as they claim to do, they actually
impose their own theological system upon Scripture and force
it to comply with their beliefs.

As evidence for this I advance, first, the fact that their *New
World Translation* of the Bible is by no means an objective render-
ing of the sacred text into modern English, but is *a biased translation in which many of the peculiar teachings of the Watchtower
Society are smuggled into the text of the Bible itself.*   The Watchtower Society, for example, has intruded into the *New World Trans-
lation* its own peculiar teaching about the Holy Spirit.   Jehovah's
Witnesses deny both the personality and the deity of the Holy
Spirit, defining the Holy Spirit as "the invisible active force of
Almighty God which moves his servants to do his will."[76]   So
pervasively has this teaching been incorporated into the *New
World Translation* that no person reading this Bible without previ-
ous theological training would ever get the impression that the
Holy Spirit is a divine Person.

Let us observe how this is done.   Though we are not told why
the *New World Translation* capitalizes words which have to do
with God, we may assume that they do so as a means of designat-

[73] *Ibid.*, p. 9.
[74] *Ibid.*, p. 121.
[75] *Ibid.*, pp. 11-18.
[76] *Ibid.*, p. 108.

ing deity (for example, God, Lord Jehovah, Rock, King, Shepherd, and so on). As is well known, Jehovah's Witnesses deny the full deity of Jesus Christ, maintaining that Christ is "a god" but not "Jehovah God," that He is not equal to the Father, and that He is not the Second Person of the Holy Trinity. It is, however, quite striking that the *New World Translation* capitalizes various titles which designate Jesus Christ: for example, Word (Jn. 1:1, 14), Son (Mt. 11:27), Saviour (Lk. 2:11), and Lord (Jn. 20:28). The capitalization of these titles presumably indicates that, though Christ is not recognized as equal to the Father, He is nevertheless honored as the highest of all God's creatures.

Against this background it is highly significant that the word *spirit,* when used to designate the Holy Spirit, is never capitalized in the *New World Translation.* In Matthew 28:19, for example, we read, "Go therefore and make disciples of people of all the nations, baptizing them in the name of the Father and of the Son and of the holy spirit." By this type of translation Jehovah's Witnesses are affirming that they refuse to ascribe to the Holy Spirit even the honor paid to Christ as the highest of all God's creatures. This rendering thus not only denies the deity of the Holy Spirit, but even denies His equality with Jesus Christ, who is considered inferior to the Father. A comparable passage is II Corinthians 13:14, "The undeserved kindness of the Lord Jesus Christ and the love of God and the sharing in the holy spirit be with all of YOU."[77] To cite a few more examples, the words *spirit* or *holy spirit* also occur in uncapitalized form in the following passages: Isaiah 63:10 ("But they themselves rebelled and made his holy spirit feel hurt"); John 14:26 ("But the helper, the holy spirit, which the Father will send in my name, that one will teach YOU all things and bring back to YOUR minds all the things I told YOU"); Acts 8:29 ("So the spirit said to Philip: 'Approach and join yourself to this chariot' "); and I Corinthians 12:3 (". . . nobody can say: 'Jesus is Lord!' except by holy spirit").[78]

Despite their claim to be only listening to Scripture, Jehovah's

[77] *You* is printed in capitals in the *New World Translation* to indicate that the pronoun is in the plural number.

[78] One cannot appeal to the Greek text to settle the question of whether Holy Spirit ought to begin with capital letters, since in the oldest manuscripts of the New Testament all the letters of every word were capitals. The capitalization of words in a translation, therefore, reflects the judgment of the translator or editor.

Witnesses are here reinterpreting the Bible in line with their Unitarian ideas about God. Most emphatically does the Bible teach the deity of the Holy Spirit. This is evident even from the *New World Translation* of Acts 5:3-4. In this passage, after Luke has recorded Ananias' sin, he reports Peter's words to him: "Ananias, why has Satan emboldened you to play false to the holy spirit. . . . You have played false, not to men, but to God."[79] The Holy Spirit, to whom Ananias has "played false," is here unmistakably designated as being God. What clearer proof could be asked for the fact that Jehovah's Witnesses pervert the Scriptures to suit their purpose?

There is, however, another way in which Jehovah's Witnesses pervert Biblical teaching about the Holy Spirit by means of their translation of the Bible. As was noted, they also deny the personality of the Holy Spirit. This denial, too, they obtrude into their supposedly objective rendering of God's Holy Word. Let us note a few examples of this. John 14:26, in the *New World Translation,* reads as follows: "But the helper, the holy spirit which the Father will send in my name, that one will teach YOU all things and bring back to YOUR minds all the things I told YOU." The relative pronoun *which* conveys to the unsuspecting reader the thought that the "holy spirit" here spoken of is not a person but an impersonal power (since, in modern English, *whom* is used to designate a person and *which* to designate a thing).[80] The Greek, to be sure, has *ho,* which is the neuter singular form of the relative pronoun. The reason for this, however, is that the antecedent of the relative is *pneuma* (spirit), which is a neuter noun in Greek. That the Evangelist did not intend to say that the helper whom the Father would send was a thing or an impersonal force is evident from the form of the demonstrative pronoun, *ekeinos* (translated *that one* in the *New World Translation*).

---

[79] Since there are some variations between the text of the *New World Translation of the Christian Greek Scriptures* which was published in 1950 and revised in 1951 and the later edition of the entire Bible, it should be noted that all quotations from the *New World Translation* appearing in this book, unless otherwise designated, are from the 1961 edition of the *New World Translation of the Holy Scriptures.*

[80] Because *which* as a relative pronoun could be used to designate persons in 17th-century English, the King James Version of 1611 could properly render the opening words of the Lord's Prayer, "Our Father which art in heaven" (Mt. 6:9, Lk. 11:2). In modern English, however, *which* may not be used to refer to persons; hence recent versions have substituted *who* for *which* in Mt. 6:9.

Though there is a neuter singular form of this pronoun, *ekeino,* it is not the neuter form which is here used but the masculine singular form, *ekeinos.* The meaning is clear: *that one, that person,* will teach you all things. The *New World* rendering, *"which* the Father will send," is therefore a biased rendering which denies the personality of the Holy Spirit.[81]

Another example of this type of mistranslation is Romans 8:16, "The spirit itself bears witness with our spirit that we are God's children." Still another example is found in Ephesians 4:30, "Also, do not be grieving God's holy spirit, with which YOU have been sealed for a day of releasing by ransom." If any Scripture passage teaches the personality of the Holy Spirit, surely it is this one; for how can one grieve an impersonal force — say, an electrical current? Yet the New World Translation again uses *which* instead of *whom.* It should be clear by now that these impersonal renderings of pronouns referring to the Holy Spirit are not objective translations but perversions of the Bible.[82]

There are other ways in which the *New World Translation* distorts the text of Scripture. More passages of this type will be examined in detail in the Appendix. Enough evidence has been given on the preceding pages, however, to establish the point that Jehovah's Witnesses are not simply going back "to the Bible alone" when

---

[81] How would Jehovah's Witnesses explain the latter half of the verse, "that one will teach you all things," in the light of their insistence that the Holy Spirit is "the invisible active force of Almighty God"? Can an impersonal force "teach all things"?

[82] If Jehovah's Witnesses wish to justify their use of the pronoun *which* with reference to the Holy Spirit on the ground of the fact that *pneuma* is a neuter noun in Greek, we would remind them that the *New World Translation* at other times uses a masculine or feminine pronoun to refer to a neuter noun. For example, in Mt. 14:11 we read, "And his head was brought on a platter and given to the maiden (*korasion*), and she brought it to her mother." The Greek verb translated "she brought" is *eenegken,* a third person singular form. This form may be translated either as "he brought," "she brought," or "it brought." The implied subject of the verb is *korasion,* a neuter noun, meaning *little girl* or *maiden.* If a neuter noun always called for a neuter pronoun, the translation should have read, *"it* brought it to her mother." Here, however, the translators correctly interpreted the neuter noun as standing for a person, and hence rendered the clause, "and *she* brought it to her mother." We can only conclude, therefore, that when the New World translators refer to the Holy Spirit as *it* or *which,* their choice of pronouns is not based upon grammatical grounds but upon their own preconceived conception of the impersonality of the Holy Spirit.

they use their *New World Translation*, but are putting into people's hands a biased rendering of the sacred text, by means of which their heretical doctrines are subtly insinuated into the minds of unsuspecting readers.

A second ground for the assertion made above (namely, that Jehovah's Witnesses do not subject themselves to the claims of Scripture but impose their own beliefs upon Scripture, thereby forcing it to comply with their teachings) is that *their method of using Scripture is to find passages which seem to support their views, and to ignore passages which fail to provide such support.* As an example of this technique, I present their attempt to disprove the doctrine of the Trinity in *Let God Be True*.

After asserting that the doctrine of the Trinity originated not with God but with Satan, the authors of this volume adduce four Scripture passages which, so they say, are "the main scriptures used to support the trinity doctrine"[83]: I John 5:7, John 10:30, I Timothy 3:16, and John 1:1. They then proceed to show that I John 5:7 is probably spurious.[84] On this point they are correct — this verse is not found in the oldest manuscripts of the Greek New Testament and hence, though found in the King James Version, it is omitted in all the modern versions, including both the ASV and the RSV.[85] It should be added at once, however, that no reputable theologian from any evangelical denomination would use this passage today as a proof-text for the Trinity!

The authors next proceed to interpret John 10:30 ("I and the Father are one") as teaching merely that Jehovah and Christ are regarded as "one in agreement, purpose and organization."[86] What the authors fail to mention, however, is that, according to verse 31, the Jews took up stones to stone Jesus, giving as their reason for this action, "For a good work we stone thee not, but for blasphemy; and because that thou, being a man, makest thyself God" (verse 33, ASV). A mere claim of agreement in purpose with God would never have made the Jews cry "blasphemy!" The clear implication of this word, understood against

---

[83] *Let God Be True*, p. 102.
[84] *Ibid.*, p. 103.
[85] In the King James Version I John 5:7 reads, "For there are three that bear record in heaven, the Father, the Word, and the Holy Ghost: and these three are one." Though these later versions do have a verse which is called verse 7, the words which comprise this verse were part of verse 6 in the King James Version.
[86] *Ibid.*, p. 104.

the background of Jewish monotheism, is that the Jews understood Jesus to be claiming full equality with God the Father.

The authors of *Let God Be True* next cite I Timothy 3:16.
Here the King James Version reads, "And without controversy
great is the mystery of godliness: God was manifest in the flesh
. . . ." The authors reject this reading in favor of the rendering
found in the American Standard Version: "He who was mani-
fested in the flesh," adding that Moffatt has also adopted this
reading.[87] They might have added that all the modern translations (including the RSV, the New English, the Berkeley Version,
and Phillips) have "he who" instead of "God," because the
manuscript evidence for the former reading is much stronger than
that for the latter. The above facts should make it clear that the
churches which confess the doctrine of the Trinity do not base
this tenet upon the older rendering of I Timothy 3:16, as Jehovah's Witnesses claim.

The last passage adduced as supporting the Trinity doctrine is
John 1:1. In agreement with the *Emphatic Diaglott*[88] and the
New World Translation, the authors render the last part of this
verse, "and the Word was a god." In the Appendix it will be
demonstrated that this rendering of the Greek text is a mistranslation. Suffice it to say here that the entire argumentation of this
paragraph is based on this mistranslation.[89]

After discussing these four passages, the authors of *Let God be
True* go on: "In the four scriptures which the clergy erroneously
quote as supporting the trinity. . . ."[90] This assertion, however,
is quite misleading, since no reputable "clergyman" or theologian
today who accepts the Trinity would use I John 5:7 in the King
James Version as a proof for that doctrine, and since no modern
version of the New Testament contains the reading of I Timothy
3:16 to which Jehovah's Witnesses object.

Confusion is worse confounded when the authors say, "Therefore, if, as claimed, it [the doctrine of the Trinity] is the 'central
doctrine of the Christian religion,' it is passing strange that this

[87] *Ibid.,* pp. 104-105.
[88] An interlinear Greek Testament, originally published in 1864 by
Benjamin Wilson, a self-educated newspaper editor of Geneva, Illinois.
Because many of Mr. Wilson's theological conceptions were similar to
Watchtower teachings, the Watchtower Society now publishes the *Emphatic Diaglott.*
[89] *Let God Be True,* p. 106.
[90] *Ibid.,* p. 107.

complicated, confusing doctrine received no attention by Christ Jesus, by way of explanation or teaching."[91]   The authors are here guilty of deliberate misrepresentation, for they have failed even so much as to mention the Great Commission of Matthew 28:19, where Jesus clearly teaches the Trinity: "Go ye therefore, and make disciples of all the nations, baptizing them into the name of the Father and of the Son and of the Holy Spirit" (ASV).   Nor has any mention been made by them in this chapter of the Apostolic Benediction of II Corinthians 13:14, the Trinitarian implications of which are quite obvious: "The grace of the Lord Jesus Christ, and the love of God, and the communion of the Holy Spirit, be with you all" (ASV).   Neither has there been the slightest reference to I Peter 1:1 and 2, a passage which gives equal honor to all three Persons of the Trinity: "Peter, an apostle of Jesus Christ, to the elect who are so-journers of the Dispersion . . . according to the foreknowledge of God the Father, in sanctification of the Spirit, unto obedience and sprinkling of the blood of Jesus Christ. . ." (ASV).

Many more passages could be quoted to show that the Bible definitely does teach the doctrine of the Trinity; passages of this sort can easily be found in any standard evangelical textbook of Christian doctrine.   Enough of these passages have been cited above, however, to demonstrate that, in "proving" their doctrines from Scripture, the Witnesses deliberately select passages which can be twisted so that they seem to favor their views, while disregarding other texts which fail to support their views.   Again we see that, instead of listening to Scripture, Jehovah's Witnesses impose their own ideas upon Scripture.

A third ground for the above-mentioned charge is *the organization's insistence that their adherents may only understand the Scriptures as these are interpreted by the leaders of the Watchtower Society.*   Though ostensibly Watchtower leaders claim the Bible alone as their sole source of authority, actually they say to their adherents: You must understand the Bible as we tell you to, or else leave the movement and thus run the risk of everlasting destruction!   For proof of this accusation I advance the following evidence:

(1) Charles Taze Russell affirmed that anyone who studied only the Bible, without the aid of his *Studies in the Scriptures*, would soon be in spiritual darkness.[92]

---

[91] *Ibid.*, p. 111.   [92] See above, p. 13.

(2) During the 1890's, while Mrs. C. T. Russell was an associate editor of the *Watch Tower* magazine, she tried to

> secure a stronger voice in directing what should appear in the *Watch Tower*. . . . When Mrs. Russell realized that no article of hers would be acceptable for publication unless it was consistent with the Scriptural views expressed in the *Watch Tower*, she became greatly disturbed and her growing resentment led her eventually to sever her relationship with the society and also with her husband.[93]

Well might she be disturbed and resentful! For the editorial policy of the magazine was obviously this: Whatever you write must agree wholly with the interpretation of Scripture taught by the group in control; if it does not, your contribution will not be accepted.

(3) In 1909 certain leaders of study classes were asking that *Watch Tower* publications should no longer be referred to in their meetings, but only the Bible. Russell himself replied to this suggestion in a *Watch Tower* article:

> This [the suggestion just made] sounded loyal to God's Word; but it was not so. It was merely the effort of those teachers to come between the people of God and the *Divinely provided light upon God's Word*.[94]

A moment's reflection on the implications of these words will reveal that, according to Russell himself, the interpretations of the Bible furnished by *Watch Tower* writers are not at all in the category of helpful but fallible guides for the understanding of Scripture. On the contrary, these interpretations are alleged to be "the Divinely provided light upon God's Word." Surely at this point we are not far removed from the position of the Mormons, who affirm that God gave His people additional revelations through Joseph Smith which are determinative for the proper understanding of the Bible.

(4) To meet the possible objection that what has been described above may have been true in Russell's day but is no longer true today, let us see what *Let God Be True* has to say about this question. After quoting Luke 12:37, the authors of this book go on to say that Jesus Christ is today the provider of spiritual food for his people and that he does so "through a visible instrument or agency on earth

---

[93] *Jehovah's Witnesses in the Divine Purpose*, p. 45.
[94] *Watch Tower*, 1909, p. 371; quoted in *Jehovah's Witnesses in the Divine Purpose*, p. 46 (the italics are Russell's).

used to publish it [this spiritual food] to his slaves."[95] Matthew 24: 45-47 is then quoted in the *New World Translation*: "Who really is the faithful and discreet slave whom his master appointed over his domestics to give them their food at the proper time? Happy is that slave if his master on arriving finds him doing so. Truly I say to you, He will appoint him over all his belongings." Now follows this statement:

> This clearly shows that the Master would use *one* organization, and not a multitude of diverse and conflicting sects, to distribute his message. The "faithful and discreet slave" is a company following the example of their Leader. That "slave" is the remnant of Christ's spiritual brothers. God's prophet identifies these spiritual Israelites, saying: "Ye are my witnesses, saith Jehovah, and my *servant* whom I have chosen" (Isa. 43: 10).
>
> From and after A.D. 1918 this "slave" class has proclaimed God's message to Christendom which still feeds on the religious traditions of men. The truth so proclaimed does a dividing work, as foretold, the ones accepting the truth being taken to the place of security, and the others abandoned. Those who have been favored to comprehend what is taking place, and who have taken their stand for Jehovah's Theocracy, have unspeakable joy now. The light of his truth is not confined to a small place, or one corner of the globe. Its proclamation is world-wide. In the thirty-three years from 1919 to 1952 inclusive Jehovah's Witnesses distributed more than half a billion bound books and booklets, hundreds of millions of magazines, tracts and leaflets, and delivered hundreds of millions of oral testimonies, in over 90 languages.[96]

As we study this quotation, several points become clear:

(1) The "faithful and discreet slave" in Jesus' parable is understood as designating an organization, namely, the "remnant of Christ's spiritual brothers." This means, in Jehovah-Witness terminology, the "anointed class," or 144,000, who play a leading role in directing the Watchtower Society and who hold all the more important offices.[97]

---

[95] *Let God Be True,* rev. ed. of 1952, p. 199.
[96] *Ibid.,* p. 200.
[97] *Ibid.,* p. 303. How these authors have come to apply the term "faithful and discreet slave" to an organization is one of the mysteries of Jehovah-Witness exegesis. In earlier days the expression was applied by this group to C. T. Russell. It was during Rutherford's time that the term came to be applied to the anointed class, this shift being, in fact, the occasion for a rather serious split within the movement

(2) The "domestics" over whom the "faithful and discreet slave" is placed are, apparently, the "other sheep," or "great crowd" — Jehovah's Witnesses who do not belong to the "anointed class," but who take an active part in the work.[98]

(3) The great task of the "anointed class" is that of providing spiritual food for the "other sheep." This implies that the "other sheep" must constantly look to the "anointed class" for the proper interpretation of the Bible and that they are not allowed to engage in any independent investigation of the Scriptures.

(4) The "spiritual food" which the "anointed class" provides is "his [Christ's] message," "God's message" [in distinction from "the religious traditions of men"], "his [God's] truth." This truth is of decisive importance since all those who accept it will find spiritual security, whereas those who do not accept it will be abandoned by God.

(5) It is this truth which is being disseminated throughout the world by means of the various publications of the Watchtower Society and by means of the oral testimonies of its members.

It is now quite evident that, despite the claim of this movement to depend on the Bible alone, the real source of authority for Jehovah's Witnesses is the interpretation of the Bible handed down by the "anointed class" at Watchtower headquarters. To use their own language, the Witnesses insist that the Watchtower Society is "the instrument or channel being used by Jehovah to teach his people on earth."[99] All Christian groups outside their fold are thus alleged to be walking in darkness, no matter how diligently they may study the Scriptures; only the Jehovah's Witnesses are said to be walking in the light, since their "anointed class" is God's channel of enlightenment for all people on earth.[100]

Instead of really listening to Scripture, therefore, Jehovah's Witnesses superimpose their own system of interpretation on the Bible, allowing it to say only what they want it to say. As an

---

(*Jehovah's Witness in the Divine Purpose,* pp. 69ff.). Actually, it will be apparent to any careful reader that Jesus in this parable is not referring to any earthly organization at all, but to spiritual overseers over God's people (like pastors or teachers), considered as individuals, who are either faithful or unfaithful to their task.

[98] This point is made clear in a discussion of this passage found in another Watchtower publication: *Qualified to be Ministers,* p. 353. See also *New Heavens and a New Earth,* 1953, p. 260.

[99] *Qualified to be Ministers,* p. 318.

[100] Yet, in *Let God Be True,* pp. 11-18, the authors solemnly claim to recognize no second source of authority next to the Bible!

example of this type of treatment of Scripture, I present their interpretation of Romans 13:1-7. From the earliest years of the Christian era this passage has been understood as applying to earthly governments and as teaching that lawfully appointed civil magistrates have been ordained by God. The reference to the sword in the ruler's hand (v. 4) and to the payment of tribute (v. 6) make it quite clear that the Apostle Paul was here discussing the believer's attitude toward governmental authorities. One wonders how, in the light of this passage, Jehovah's Witnesses can justify their insistence that all governmental authorities are part of the devil's organization.

Their reply is really quite simple: the church has never properly understood Romans 13!

> In 1929 the clear light broke forth. That year *The Watchtower* published the Scriptural exposition of Romans chapter 13. It showed that Jehovah God and Christ Jesus, rather than worldly rulers and governors, are "The Higher Powers". . . .[101]

In another volume we are told that the submission which Romans 13 tells us to render to Jehovah God and Jesus Christ, as our "Superior Authorities," includes "Theocratic submission" to those who have divine authority in the Theocratic organization — in other words, to the "anointed class."[102] The authors of *This Means Everlasting Life* further inform us that the *sword* of verse 4 is to be understood in a symbolic sense, as standing for God's power of executing judgment.[103] Most inconsistently, however, the *tribute* of verse 6 is interpreted quite literally, as referring to the payment of taxes to the government![104] Why the sword is to be understood symbolically and the tribute must be interpreted literally, we are not told. Is further proof required to show that Jehovah's Witnesses do not arrive at their interpretations of Scripture by thorough, diligent, contextual study of the Word, but by imposing their preconceived ideas upon the Word?

Kurt Hutten, one of the ablest students of the cults in our time, has aptly summed up the Witnesses' claim to be Jehovah's sole channel of truth in the following words:

---

[101] *The Truth Shall Make You Free*, 1943, p. 312. See also *Let God Be True*, p. 248, and *What Has Religion Done for Mankind?*, 1951, p. 292. Note the implication of the statement quoted above: previous to 1929 no one properly understood this passage!

[102] *This Means Everlasting Life*, 1950, p. 203.

[103] *Ibid.*, p. 199.

[104] *Ibid.*, p. 200.

The members of the [Jehovah-Witness] organization are obligated to unconditional obedience. This obligation includes the duty of accepting the word of God only in the interpretation offered them by the Brooklyn publications. The Watchtower Society has divine authority and hence also possesses a monopoly on the truth and on the proper proclamation of the Gospel. It is forbidden to nourish oneself from other sources or to think one's own thoughts. Those who do this disregard "the light which comes to them through God's channel with reference to His Word," and imply that *The Watchtower* is not sufficient for our time." They thereby commit an offense which entails disastrous consequences, and are by Jehovah not reckoned as belonging to the "sheep" but to the "goats." For to despise the Theocratic organization is to despise Jesus Christ.[105]

METHOD OF INTERPRETING SCRIPTURE

It is, of course, conceivable that someone might say, Granted that the Jehovah's Witnesses recognize a superior source of authority in their own Watchtower publications, might it not be possible that the Watchtower publication staff does a fairly competent job of interpreting Scripture? By way of anticipating this type of question, I should like to describe briefly the methods of Scriptural interpretation used by this group. As we examine these methods, it will again become quite clear that Jehovah's Witnesses do not really subject themselves to the authority of God's Word, but simply manipulate the Scriptures so as to force them to agree with Watchtower teachings.

The interpretation of Scripture found in Jehovah-Witness publications is often characterized by *absurd literalism*. For example, Jehovah's Witnesses prohibit their members from receiving blood

---

[105] *Seher, Gruebler, Enthusiasten*, 6th ed. (Stuttgart: Quell-Verlag, 1960), p. 105 [translation mine]. It is significant that this complete domination of Scripture interpretation by Watchtower leaders is precisely what William J. Schnell experienced during his thirty years with the movement. See, e.g., p. 43 of his *Thirty Years a Watchtower Slave*, where he explains how the leaders of the society put themselves "into the sole position of giving the Organization's instructions on how to worship, what to worship with, and what to believe." Note also what is said by him on p. 107 about the indoctrination methods of the society whereby "their brain [that of the Jonadabs or 'other sheep'] became totally washed of any other ideas they might ever have loosely held about the Bible, themselves, or other people. Their own thoughts were thus replaced by a narrow sphere or circumscribed area of thought, or as the Watch Tower put it, a 'channel.' "

transfusions, justifying this prohibition by an appeal to Scripture passages which forbid the eating of blood. A sample of the type of passage involved is Leviticus 17:14, ". . . I said unto the children of Israel, Ye shall eat the blood of no manner of flesh. . . .[106] On the basis of Biblical passages of this sort they assert that blood transfusion is a "feeding upon blood," and is therefore "an unscriptural practice."[107] Certain that they have thus discerned Jehovah's will in this matter, Jehovah's Witnesses will deliberately let a loved one die rather than to permit a blood transfusion.[108]

Another example of absurd literalism is mentioned by Charles S. Braden: Jehovah's Witnesses forbid the use of Christmas trees on the basis of Jeremiah 10:3 and 4, ". . . The customs of the peoples are vanity; for one cutteth a tree out of the forest, the work of the hands of the workman with the axe. They deck it with silver and with gold. . . ." This must be, so they say, a Biblical reference to the Christmas tree; since verse 2 of this chapter says, "Learn not the way of the nations," it is obvious that the Christmas tree stands condemned![109]

---

[106] Other Old Testament passages adduced by them in this connection include Gen. 9:3-5; Lev. 7:26, 27; Lev. 17:10-12; Deut. 12:16. It is added that the prohibition of blood was also enjoined upon Christians in New Testament times, according to Acts 15:28, 29 (*Make Sure of All Things,* rev. ed., 1957, p. 47).

[107] *Ibid.*

[108] It should be observed, however, that (1) the blood which was prohibited in the Levitical laws was not human blood but animal blood; (2) what was forbidden was the eating of this blood with the mouth — which is something quite different from receiving blood into one's veins as a medicinal measure; (3) the reason for this Old Testament prohibition is stated in Lev. 17:11, namely, that God had appointed the blood of animals as a means of making atonement, and that therefore such blood was not to be used as food (cf. C. F. Keil and F. Delitzsch, *Commentary on the Pentateuch* [Edinburgh: Clark, 1891], II, 410); and (4) the reason why Gentile Christians were asked to abstain from blood, according to Acts 15:20 and 29, was that they might not give offense to Jewish Christians, who at this time still shrank with horror from the eating of blood (cf. F. F. Bruce, *Commentary on Acts* [Grand Rapids: Eerdmans, 1955], and Lenski, *ad loc.*). It is quite clear, therefore, that neither the Old Testament nor the New Testament passages adduced by Jehovah's Witnesses on this matter have anything to do with the current medical practice of blood transfusion. (For fuller treatment of this question, see Martin and Klann, *op. cit.,* pp. 115-26).

[109] *These Also Believe,* p. 379 (unfortunately, Dr. Braden does not mention the source of his information). It will be quite clear to even a casual reader of Jeremiah 10, however, that what is forbidden and ridiculed in vv. 3-5 is the making of wooden idols.

These are but two examples of Jehovah-Witness literalism; many more could be given. It must not be inferred, however, that Jehovah's Witnesses always interpret the Bible literally. On the contrary, they are quite ready to spiritualize Scripture passages when such spiritualization fits into their preconceived ideas. For example, they spiritualize the sword in Romans 13:4,[110] and the twelve tribes in Revelation 7:4-8.[111] They are opposed to the literal interpretation of Christ's physical resurrection,[112] of prophecies concerning the return of the Jews to their land,[113] and of prophecies regarding Christ's physical and visible return to earth.[114]

At other times the interpretation of Scripture found in Jehovah-Witness publications is characterized by *absurd typology.* So, for example, it is said that Noah in the Old Testament typified Jesus Christ; that Noah's wife pictured the "bride of Christ," that is, the "Christian congregation of 144,000 anointed members"; that Noah's three sons and three daughters-in-law pictured the "great crowd" (namely, the "other sheep," or larger class of Jehovah-Witness adherents). The ark pictured the "new system of things according to the new covenant mediated by Jesus Christ." The flood symbolized the coming Battle of Armageddon.[115]

Another example of absurd typology is the Jehovah-Witness interpretation of the Parable of the Rich Man and Lazarus, found in Luke 16:19-31. This parable, we are told, tells us nothing about the state or condition of people after death, but simply pictures two classes existing on earth today:

> The rich man represents the ultraselfish class of the clergy of Christendom, who are now afar off from God and dead to his favor and service and tormented by the Kingdom truth proclaimed. Lazarus depicts the faithful remnant of the "body

110 See above, p. 36.
111 *Let God Be True,* p. 130. Jehovah's Witnesses take literally the number 144,000 mentioned in these verses, but symbolically the distribution of these 144,000 into the twelve tribes of Israel.
112 *Ibid.,* p. 40.
113 *Ibid.,* p. 217.
114 *Ibid.,* pp. 197ff.
115 *New Heavens and a New Earth,* pp. 310-11; cf. *You May Survive Armageddon into God's New World,* 1955, p. 292; and *The Truth Shall Make You Free,* 1943, pp. 323-27. To see Noah as a type of Christ, and Noah's family as a type of the church is, of course, quite in harmony with Biblical typology. But by what stretch of the imagination are we justified in separating Noah's wife from Noah's children, as standing for two different groups within the church?

of Christ." These, on being delivered from modern Babylon since 1919, receive God's favor, pictured by the "bosom position of Abraham," and are comforted through his Word.[116]

William G. Schnell gives a further example of this kind of typology. In 1931, he claims, the Watchtower Society interpreted the Parable of the Laborers in the Vineyard, found in Matthew 20:1-16, as follows: the twelve hours of the parable stood for the twelve years which had elapsed since 1919 (when the society had received a new lease on life after the discharge of its leaders from prison). The shilling which every laborer received, regardless of the length of time he had served, stood for the new name which each member of the organization received that year, whether he had been with the movement from the beginning or had just joined: the name *Jehovah's Witness!*[117]

A third common characteristic of Jehovah-Witness Scripture study is what might be called *"knight-jump exegesis."* Kurt Hutten, who devotes several pages to an analysis of Watchtower exegetical methods,[118] has coined this expression to describe the way Witnesses jump from one part of the Bible to another, with utter disregard of context, to "prove" their points.[119] He goes on to affirm that the Bible should be interpreted in an organic fashion, in a manner which does full justice to the differences between Old and New Testament, between poetic books and prophetic books, between histories and epistles, and which takes into account the fact that revelation is progressive — that it advances from lesser to greater clarity. Since Jehovah's Witnesses cannot draw their teachings from the Bible when so interpreted, however, they must, Hutten continues, resort to "knight-jump" methods to arrive at their conclusions.[120] The Bible, for them, is like a flat surface in which every text has equal value.

> They [Jehovah's Witnesses] . . . can jump blithely from a passage in the Pentateuch to a passage in the prophets or in the book of Revelation. They can thus draw their lines in all di-

[116] *Let God Be True*, p. 98. The reader is also referred to *What Has Religion Done for Mankind?*, 1951, pp. 246-56 and 302-12, for a fuller discussion of this parable.
[117] *Thirty Years a Watchtower Slave*, p. 97.
[118] *Seher, Gruebler, Enthusiasten*, pp. 119-25.
[119] *"Der Roesselsprung," ibid.*, p. 120. A knight-jump in chess is a move of three squares over the chessboard so that the piece passes over any adjacent square whether occupied or not, and alights on a square of different color from that which it started.
[120] *Ibid.*, pp. 121-22.

rections [*kreuz und quer*] through the Bible, gleefully combine them in zigzag fashion, and put them together again in the most fantastic way.[121]

Hutten also compares their method of using Scripture to that of children building various structures with building blocks, the Bible being, for the Witnesses, the box which contains the blocks. The only difference, so the author continues, is that, whereas children do this type of thing in a playful spirit, being perfectly ready to knock down their houses as soon as (or very soon after) they have built them, Jehovah's Witnesses use this method in dead earnest, believing that they are thus honoring the revelation of God![122]

An outstanding example of this method of Bible interpretation is their manner of arriving at the date 1914 as the year when Christ's Kingdom was established. Jehovah's Witnesses claim that "Christ the Messiah did not set up God's kingdom at his first advent or at once after ascending to heaven."[123] How, then, can we determine the time when the kingdom was established? From Luke 21:24 it is learned that "Jerusalem will be trampled on by the nations, until the appointed times of the nations are fulfilled" (NWT).[124] The "appointed times of the nations," it is said, "indicated a period in which there would be no representative government of Jehovah on earth, such as the kingdom of Israel was; but the Gentile nations would dominate the earth."[125] These times were running already in Jesus' day, since Jerusalem was then in bondage to Rome. When, then, had these "times of the nations" begun? In 607 B.C., when Israel, which was a theocracy, lost her sovereignty and was carried away to Babylon.[126]

---

[121] *Ibid.*, p. 121 [translation mine].

[122] *Ibid.*, pp. 121-22.

[123] *The Truth Shall Make You Free*, p. 241.

[124] The abbreviation NWT will be used from now on for the 1961 edition of the *New World Translation*.

[125] *Let God Be True*, p. 250.

[126] *Ibid.*, pp. 250-51. In *Paradise Lost* (this abbreviation will be used from now on for *From Paradise Lost to Paradise Regained*), 1958, p. 172, it is specifically stated: "The king of Babylon took Zedekiah off 'Jehovah's throne' in the year 607 B.C. and laid his city and territory desolate. So that year God's earthly kingdom ended. And that year, 607 B.C., the 'appointed times of the nations' began." Unfortunately, however, the facts do not bear out this assertion, which is pivotal for Jehovah-Witness chronology. Old Testament scholars are virtually unanimous in dating the capture of Zedekiah and the fall of Jerusalem, not in 607 B.C., but in 587 or 586 B.C. (cf. J. D. Douglas, ed., *The*

From Daniel 7:14, it is said, we learn that Christ was to receive a kingdom which will never be destroyed. It is then naively added, "When would Christ receive this never-to-be-destroyed kingdom? At the end of the 'appointed times of the nations.' "[127]

When, then, will these "appointed times of the nations" end? For the answer we switch to Daniel 4, which contains the account of Nebuchadnezzar's dream of the tree and his subsequent period of living like a beast of the field. This vision, we are told, was a "prophetic vision . . . concerning the times of the nations and the restoration of Jehovah's Theocracy."[128] Nebuchadnezzar is told that after he shall have been reduced to the status of a beast, "seven times" shall pass over him; following this his kingdom shall be restored to him (Dan. 4:25-26). These "seven times," it is said, depict symbolically the length of the "times of the nations."[129]

How, then, do we determine the length of these "seven times"? In the case of Nebuchadnezzar they meant seven literal years. Obviously this cannot be the prophetic meaning of the "seven times," for then Christ would have ascended his throne already in the Old Testament era. When we compare Revelation 12:6 with Revelation 12:14, however, we learn that "a time, and times, and half a time" is equivalent to 1260 days. Obviously, a time, and times, and half a time" are three and a half times. But three and a half times constitute half of seven times; hence seven times must equal twice 1260 days, or 2,520 days.[130]

We are still not through with our calculation, however, since 2,520 literal days would only bring us seven years beyond the beginning of the "appointed times of the nations." There must be some deeper meaning hidden in this figure of 2,520 days. We find this deeper meaning when we turn to Ezekiel 4:6. There we read, in the King James Version, "I have appointed thee every day for a year."[131] Thus we have our clue:

New Bible Dictionary, p. 1357; *The Westminster Dictionary of the Bible*, p. 108; *The Westminster Historical Atlas to the Bible*, p. 15; and Merrill F. Unger, *Archaeology of the Old Testament*, p. 284).

[127] *Paradise Lost*, p. 173.

[128] *Let God Be True*, p. 251. How the Watchtower editorial staff can be so sure that this vision, which was given to Nebuchadnezzar to reveal what God was about to do to him and to his kingdom, pertains to the "times of the nations," we are not told.

[129] *Ibid.*, p. 251; cf. pp. 251-54.

[130] *Ibid.*, p. 252.

[131] Even the casual reader of this chapter will note that the expression

By applying this divine rule the 2,520 days means 2,520 years. Therefore, since God's typical kingdom with its capital at Jerusalem ceased to exist in the autumn of 607 B.C., then, by counting the appointed times from that date, the 2,520 years extend to the autumn of A.D. 1914.[132]

Thus, by a calculation which involves a conglomeration of figures derived with great ingenuity from assorted passages taken from Luke, Daniel, Revelation, and Ezekiel, we have arrived at the year 1914. Here is "knight-jump exegesis" with a vengeance! Yet Jehovah's Witnesses assure us that by this type of procedure they are listening to the Word of God instead of to the traditions of men!

A fourth characteristic of Jehovah-Witness exegesis is what we might call the *"rear-view method" of interpreting prophecy.* Hutten indicates that much of their prophetic interpretation rests upon a rather primitive kind of trick: they first pounce on certain happenings in the recent past, then find some Biblical texts which can somehow be made to fit these events, after which they triumphantly point to the events in question as "fulfilled prophecies."[133]

As an example of this technique, I suggest the Jehovah-Witness interpretation of Revelation 11:11-13. This passage describes the two witnesses who, after having been killed, were revived again. The Witnesses say this prophecy was fulfilled in 1919, when Judge Rutherford and other leaders of the movement were released from prison and thus enabled to resume their witnessing activities![134]

Another example of this type of "rear-view" exegesis is the Jehovah-Witness explanation of Revelation 17:3-6. This passage depicts a woman sitting on a scarlet-colored beast, on whose forehead has been written the name, "Babylon the Great, the mother of the harlots and of the disgusting things of the earth" (NWT). Jehovah's Witnesses interpret this woman as standing for "the visible organization of the religious heads of heathendom

---

quoted above designates the meaning of the symbolic action the prophet is commanded to engage in: each day the prophet lies on his side stands for a year in the history of the house of Israel or the house of Judah. To draw from this passage a rule applicable to a figure derived from the book of Revelation is, to say the least, dubious exegesis!

[132] *Let God Be True,* p. 252.

[133] *Seher, Gruebler, Enthusiasten,* p. 123.

[134] *You May Survive Armageddon* [this abbreviation will be used from now on for *You May Survive Armageddon into God's New World*], pp. 116-120. See also *New Heavens and a New Earth,* pp. 255-56.

and Christendom."[135]   The beast the woman rides, it is further said, is

> this peace beast, formerly known as the League of Nations but now since its reappearance in 1945 the United Nations. Its having sixty member nations in 1951 was well symbolized in the peace beast's having seven heads and ten horns.[136]

In *Let God Be True* we are given a further reason why this identification of the beast with the present-day United Nations organization must be true: "As for that many-membered beastly association of nations, the 'wild beast that you saw was, but is not [during World War II], and yet is destined to ascend out of the abyss [as the United Nations]'."[137]

Having briefly examined some typical methods of Scripture interpretation used by Jehovah's Witnesses, we conclude that they do not really subject themselves to the authority of the Bible alone, apart from human traditions, as they claim to do. Rather, as we now see more clearly, their very method of interpreting the Scriptures makes it impossible for them really to listen to God's Word. Given the methods described above, one can draw from the Bible virtually any doctrine his imagination can concoct. These doctrines may be interesting, novel, and appealing — but they suffer from one fatal defect: they do not rest upon the authority of God's Word, but upon the fabrications of man's mind!

---

[135] *What Has Religion Done for Mankind?*, 1951, p. 328. Note the utterly arbitrary way in which all heathen religions and all forms of Christianity are lumped together as constituting "the great whore" of Rev. 17. For Jehovah's Witnesses, therefore, there is no religiously significant difference between, say, a Nigerian animist and a devout Lutheran Christian.

[136] *Ibid.*, pp. 328-29. How 60 member nations are pictured by 7 heads and 10 horns we are not told.

[137] P. 258. The words between single quotation marks have been quoted from Revelation 17:8 in the 1951 ed. of the NWT, comments between brackets having been inserted by the authors of *Let God Be True*. For Jehovah's Witnesses, therefore, the fact that the beast is described as one that "was, is not, and is destined to ascend out of the abyss" proves conclusively that this Scripture passage predicted the rise of the League of Nations, its disappearance, and the subsequent rise of the United Nations!

III. Doctrines

DOCTRINE OF GOD

THE BEING OF GOD

The Trinity. As is well known, Jehovah's Witnesses reject the doctrine of the Trinity. They claim, in fact, that this doctrine originated with the ancient Babylonians at about 2200 B.C.[138] It is said that the Babylonians had a kind of divine triad: Cush, the father; Semiramis, the mother (Cush's wife); and Nimrod, the first ruler of Babylon, who was the son of Semiramis but later became her husband. Since all three of these individuals were deified by the Babylonians, this is where the idea of the trinity originated.[139] Later the Hindus, it is claimed, borrowed this idea of a divine triad from the Babylonians. In the Hindu religion this trinity assumed the following form: Brahma the Creator, Vishnu the Preserver, and Siva the Destroyer. These three together composed the one god Brahm.[140] There was even a kind of trinity in Egypt: the goddess Isis, her sister Nephthys, and Osiris, the son of Nephthys, who was adopted by Isis as her son, but who also became Isis's husband.[141] We conclude, it is said, that the doctrine of the trinity had its origin in the demon-religions of ancient Baby-

---

138 *Make Sure of All Things*, p. 386.
139 *Religion for Mankind* [this abbreviation will be used from now on for *What Has Religion Done for Mankind?*], pp. 92-95. On p. 95 it is added that, since Nimrod had married his mother, one could say that he was his own father and his own son. Thus, it is said, the way was prepared for the doctrine of the trinity.
140 *Ibid.*, p. 193.
141 *Ibid.*, p. 109.

lon, India, and Egypt. "The obvious conclusion is, therefore, that Satan is the originator of the Trinity doctrine."[142]

According to Jehovah's Witnesses, the only true God, in one person, is Jehovah. Before He began to create, Jehovah was all alone in universal space.[143] It is recognized that the name *Elohim* is also applied to God in the Old Testament; it is, in fact, specifically affirmed that the plural form of *Elohim* does not denote the persons of the Trinity but is a plural of majesty, which describes a single person.[144] The Witnesses claim, however, that Jehovah, which they prefer to use, is God's true and exclusive name. While granting that perhaps this name should be pronounced *Yahweh,* they favor the form *Jehovah* because this is the most familiar and popular way of rendering the divine name.[145]

This divine name is therefore consistently rendered *Jehovah* in the Old Testament section of the *New World Translation* — a practice to which no exception can be taken, particularly since this was also done by the translators of the American Standard Version. Without any Scriptural warrant whatsoever, however, Jehovah's Witnesses have also introduced the name Jehovah 237 times into the text of the *New World Translation* of the New Testament.[146]

[142] *Let God Be True,* p. 101.
[143] *Ibid.,* p. 25.
[144] *New Heavens and a New Earth,* pp. 35-36.
[145] *Let God Be True,* p. 23; *New World Translation of the Christian Greek Scriptures,* 1951 ed., pp. 10, 25.
[146] *New World Translation of the Christian Greek Scriptures,* p. 24. On what basis do they justify this practice? Their argument runs as follows: A papyrus manuscript of the second half of Deuteronomy in the LXX translation has recently been found, which has been dated from the second or first century B.C. This manuscript, called Papyrus Fouad 266, consistently has the tetragrammaton (JHVH, the Hebrew form rendered Jehovah in the ASV) in Aramaic characters for the divine name instead of the common renderings of the name: *Kurios* (Lord) or *Theos* (God). From this fact it is concluded that the original manuscripts of the LXX, which were written in the 3rd and 2nd centuries B.C., also must have had the divine name in its tetragrammaton form instead of in the forms *Kurios* or *Theos,* and it is implied that later copyists of the LXX deliberately substituted *Kurios* or *Theos* for the tetragrammaton (pp. 11-12). This being so, Christ and his disciples must have had copies of the LXX which had the divine name in its tetragrammaton form (p. 12). The writers of the New Testament, therefore, must have used the tetragrammaton for the divine name in their Greek writings, which would include the books of the New Testament (p. 18). Hence it is obvious that the text of the New Testament has been tampered with and that copyists have eliminated the tetragramma-

Jehovah's Witnesses deny the full deity of Jesus Christ, and his complete equality with Jehovah. He may be called *a god,* but not *Jehovah God;* he is *a mighty one* but not *almighty* as Jehovah God is.[147] He was created by Jehovah as the first son brought forth by Him; "hence he is called 'the only begotten Son' of God, for God had no partner in bringing forth his first-begotten Son."[148] Since Christ was the first creature of Jehovah, he had a beginning.[149] It is obvious therefore, that Christ is not the second person of the Trinity.[150]

As has already been stated, the Holy Spirit is, for Jehovah's Witnesses, "the invisible active force of Almighty God which moves his servants to do his will."[151] At another place it is added: "It [the Holy Spirit] is the impersonal, invisible active force that finds its source and reservoir in Jehovah God and that he uses to accomplish his will even at great distances, over light years of space."[152] The Holy Spirit is therefore neither God nor a person;

---

ton from these manuscripts, substituting for it either *Kurios* or *Theos* (p. 18). Therefore, Jehovah's Witnesses say, we are justified in replacing *Kurios* or *Theos* with the tetragrammaton (in the form *Jehovah*) in 237 instances (p. 19).

In reply, the following may be said: (1) The fact that an early fragment of the LXX used the tetragrammaton exclusively does not prove that the entire LXX text originally followed this practice. This fragment may simply have represented one type of LXX text. If the tetragrammaton were used exclusively in the original manuscripts, how do we account for its complete disappearance from the 4th and 5th century uncials of the LXX? (2) Even if the LXX did originally use the tetragrammaton, this fact would give us no warrant for tampering with the text of the New Testament which has *Kurios* or *Theos* for God but never JHVH, not even where JHVH did occur in Old Testament passages quoted (see Moulton and Geden's *Concordance to the Greek Testament* under *Kurios*). To assume that the text of the New Testament has been corrupted in 237 places *without one shred of textual evidence* is to engage in a most dangerous kind of speculation! (3) The fact, alluded to by them, that some translations of the New Testament into Hebrew use the tetragrammaton to designate God proves precisely nothing! For how otherwise would Hebrew translators render a Greek word which was originally JHVH?

[147] *Let God Be True,* pp. 32, 33.
[148] *Ibid.,* p. 32.
[149] *Ibid.,* p. 33.
[150] Further details about their view of Christ will be given under the Doctrine of Christ.
[151] *Let God Be True,* p. 108.
[152] *Let Your Name Be Sanctified,* 1961, p. 269. Note the word *reservoir,* which suggests that the Holy Spirit is a kind of substance which is stored in God.

he is merely an impersonal force — we have previously noted how Jehovah's Witnesses have insinuated this conception of the Holy Spirit into their *New World Translation*.[153]

Strictly speaking, therefore, Jehovah's Witnesses are Unitarians. For them, God exists only in one Person — the Person of Jehovah. Jesus Christ, though a person, is not a divine Person; the Holy Spirit is neither a person nor a divine Person.

The Attributes of God. The Witnesses usually speak of four attributes of Jehovah: justice, power, love, and wisdom. No attempt is made by them to distinguish between incommunicable and communicable attributes, it being specifically said that the same four attributes or qualities which are found in God are also found in man.[154]

Are any of these attributes given prominence above others? It has frequently been said that Jehovah's Witnesses minimize the love of God, and tend to exalt the power of God as His outstanding attribute. Charles Braden, for example, makes this assertion[155]; John H. Gerstner implies the same.[156] Kurt Hutten is of the opinion that the vindication of Jehovah is, for Jehovah's Witnesses, the theme of world history — a vindication which will finally reveal itself in a spectacular kind of public triumph over Satan and his hosts. What the Witnesses fail to see, he continues, is that according to Scripture God glorifies Himself especially through His love, revealed in the sending of His Son into the world to seek and to save that which was lost.[157]

What shall we say about this? To be fair to the Witnesses at this point, we must grant that they do stress the importance of the love of God. They make love, as we have seen, one of the main attributes of God. Further, in the booklet entitled *God's Way is Love,* published in 1952, great emphasis is laid on this attribute of God. We are here told, for example, that God's love is opposed to both purgatorial torment after death and eternal torment in hell (p. 12), that God showed his love in creating the universe (pp. 14-17), and in putting man into an earthly paradise of pleasure (p. 18). After Adam and Eve had sinned, God showed

---

[153] See above, pp. 27-29.
[154] *Your Will Be Done* [this abbreviation will be used from now on for *Your Will Be Done on Earth,* 1958], p. 21. On p. 191 of *Make Sure of All Things,* however, the omnipresence of Jehovah is denied.
[155] *These Also Believe,* p. 371.
[156] *Theology of the Major Sects* (Grand Rapids: Baker, 1960), p. 36.
[157] *Seher, Gruebler, Enthusiasten,* pp. 129-30.

his love for mankind by giving man the promise of Genesis 3:15 (p. 20). The Bible, we are told, is a gift of God's love (p. 22). The reign of Christ, which began in 1914, is an expression of God's love for mankind (p. 27). Even the Battle of Armageddon is an expression of God's love for man since it will be a blessing for man to have the wicked destroyed (p. 28). God's provision of redemption for mankind is said to be a manifestation of his love (p. 31). In fact, "everything God has done and will do in the future is prompted by love" (p. 13).

It is therefore not correct to say that Jehovah's Witnesses lay no stress on the love of God. It is true, however, that for them the vindication of Jehovah or of Jehovah's name is the primary purpose of world history:

> . . . Today the great issue before all heaven and earth is, Who is supreme? Who in fact and in right exercises the sovereignty over all the universe? Jehovah's primary purpose is to settle this issue. To do so means the vindication of his universal sovereignty or domination.[158]

It is further said that the great means whereby Jehovah will vindicate Himself will be the war of Armageddon and that the vindication of His reproached name is more important than the salvation of men.[159]

It should further be observed that the vindication of Jehovah is also the primary purpose for which Jesus came to earth: "After this announcement of the Kingdom Jesus went to John, showing the primary purpose for which he came to earth, namely, to bear witness to God's kingdom which will vindicate the sovereignty and holy name of Jehovah God."[160] It is granted that Jesus also came to earth to redeem man, but this is said to have been a secondary purpose:

> Thus John showed the secondary purpose for which the Son of God came to earth, namely, to die as a holy sacrifice to Jehovah God in order to cancel the sins of believing men and to free them from death's condemnation, that they might gain

[158] *Let God Be True*, pp. 27-28. See also p. 163: ". . . Vindication of Jehovah's name and sovereignty is the foremost doctrine of the Bible. . . ."
[159] *Ibid.*, p. 29. Note that, in the light of this statement, the primary purpose of Armageddon is not to reveal God's love to man but to vindicate Jehovah over against his enemies. Cf. on this point also *You May Survive Armageddon*, pp. 25-26, where it is specifically said that Armageddon will be a manifestation of God's justice rather than of His love.
[160] *Let God Be True*, p. 37.

eternal life in the righteous new world which God has promised to create.[161]

I conclude, therefore, that, though Jehovah's Witnesses do stress the love of God in various ways, in the totality of their theology Jehovah's love is subordinated to His power and His justice. For this judgment I advance the following reasons: (1) It is clearly stated by them that the vindication of Jehovah is the primary purpose of world history and of the coming of Christ. This vindication of Jehovah means that He will prove Himself superior to His enemies, both in regard to the rightness of His cause and the greatness of His power. This vindication will be dramatized especially by the great climax of world history, the Battle of Armageddon, at which He will overwhelmingly demolish His foes. (2) Even in God's plan of redemption, which is secondary to His main purpose, it is not so much the love of God for unworthy sinners which is magnified as His just recognition of the worthiness of His true followers. As will become evident when we discuss Jehovah-Witness soteriology, Jehovah's true people, whether belonging to the anointed class or to the other sheep, are chosen by Him because of their worthiness in believing on Him and in dedicating their lives to Him. During the millennium the millions who will be raised from the dead will be given a new opportunity to show their faithfulness and obedience to Jehovah, on the basis of which their final destiny will be determined. Even the way of salvation, therefore, in Jehovah-Witness theology, serves primarily to vindicate Jehovah's justice rather than to reveal His love.

THE WORKS OF GOD

Decrees. One of the first doctrines Russell doubted was predestination. It will be of interest, therefore, to see what present-day Witnesses teach about this doctrine.

Only with respect to Jesus Christ do Jehovah's Witnesses teach the predestination of an individual: "Only in the case of the chief member of the new creation did God foreordain and foreknow the individual, his only-begotten Son."[162] Having used Christ in forming the heavens and the earth, Jehovah then used

---

[161] *Ibid.,* p. 38. In the light of these quotations it would seem that God's provision of redemption for mankind as a manifestation of his love is only a secondary purpose for Christ's coming to earth.
[162] *New Heavens and a New Earth,* p. 159.

him also in forming His new creation: namely, the people that were to constitute His new nation. Of this people Jesus Christ was chosen to be the head.[163]

What about the members of this new nation?

> In the case of the others [those other than Christ] he [Jehovah] did not choose to predestinate the individuals, although he did foreordain the number of them and their nationality. But he left it open to those favored with the opportunity in his fore-ordained time to prove themselves worthy of being incorporated finally into the new creation.[164]

God foreordained the exact number of this new nation: 144,000. This number has been derived from Revelation 7:4-8, and 14:1 and 3; Jehovah's Witnesses take this number literally, but they take the fact that these 144,000, according to Revelation 7:5-8, were selected out of the twelve tribes of Israel, figuratively![165] It was therefore foreordained by Jehovah that this group would be no larger than 144,000 and that its members would be drawn from various nations.[166]

It is clear that this is not predestination in the Reformed sense or even in the Arminian sense. God has simply determined the number of people that will belong to this class, but He has not chosen them as individuals. The following passage adds the thought that God has simply determined beforehand what should be the requirements for belonging to this class:

> God has foreknowledge of the elect [another name for the 144,000]; not meaning that he chose to foreknow the individuals, but that he purposed or predestinated that there should be such an elect company. . . . He did not have to concern himself with the individuals and their names and personal identities. He simply determined beforehand or predestinated what should be the requirements for membership in this class and what standards they had to meet and what qualities they had to display.[167]

---

[163] *Ibid.*, p. 160. The "new nation" means the anointed class or 144,000. From time to time in this exposition, the distinction between "anointed class" and "other sheep" will be referred to, since one cannot understand any phase of Jehovah-Witness theology apart from this distinction. A more complete description of these two groups will be given under the Doctrine of the Church.

[164] *Ibid.*, p. 159.

[165] *Let God Be True*, p. 130.

[166] *New Heavens and a New Earth*, pp. 168-69.

[167] *The Kingdom Is at Hand*, 1944, pp. 291-92.

How about the "other sheep"? Has their number also been determined beforehand by God? No. Since Revelation 7:9 and 10 tells us about a "great crowd which no man was able to number," distinct from the 144,000 mentioned in the earlier verses of the chapter, Jehovah's Witnesses conclude that the other sheep are not limited in number. "Anyone may become one of this great crowd of sheeplike people who will gain everlasting life on a paradise earth."[168] How? By hearing the voice of the Right Shepherd and coming into the New World Society.[169] This means, of course, subjecting themselves to the Society's requirements for other sheep.

Jehovah's Witnesses thus deny that God has chosen from eternity those who are to be saved, whether they be members of the anointed class or of the other sheep. By thus rejecting divine predestination they impugn the sovereignty of God. At this point it would seem that the "vindication of Jehovah's sovereignty" is not coming off very well.

Creation. Jehovah's Witnesses affirm that God created all that exists and therefore vigorously oppose all evolutionary theories.[170] God's various creations, however, took place at various points in time.

The first creature Jehovah made was Jesus Christ. Previous to this time Jehovah had been sonless; now He for the first time became a father. Jehovah did not form Christ out of pre-existent matter or with the help of a "female principle"; He formed Christ out of nothing. Christ was therefore the only direct Son of God; hence he may be called the only-begotten Son.[171]

With the co-operation of this Son, Jehovah afterwards brought forth all His other sons.[172] In other words, Jehovah used His Son as a working partner or co-worker through whom all other things, including angels and men, were brought into existence.[173]

Next God created a realm of spirits. "The creating of the spirit realm was long before the creating of the material universe

---

[168] *Paradise Lost,* p. 195.
[169] *Ibid.,* p. 196.
[170] *Let God Be True,* Chap. 7.
[171] *New Heavens and a New Earth,* pp. 24-25. Note that the Witnesses do not recognize the kind of distinction suggested in the Nicene Creed: "begotten, not made"; for they maintain that Christ was both created by the Father and begotten by the Father.
[172] *Ibid.,* p. 25.
[173] *Ibid.,* pp. 62-63; *Let God Be True,* p. 33. Cf. *The Truth Shall Make You Free,* p. 48.

with its billions of independent galaxies like our own Milky Way."[174]   This spirit realm consisted of myriads of angels, sometimes called "sons of God" in the Bible.   Thus, in a sense, the angels are brothers of Jesus Christ, the first-created Son (who in his pre-human state was the archangel Michael).[175]   Since Satan was originally one of the spirit-sons of Jehovah, we may say that Satan, too, was originally a brother of Jesus Christ.[176]   The prophet Daniel was given a vision of hundreds of millions of angels before God's throne (Daniel 7:9, 10).   All these angels are organized and placed in various positions of service.[177]

> All together, they [the angels] form the invisible heavenly organization of Jehovah God, in complete subjection to him and lovingly obedient to him as their theocratic Head and Life-giver.   From the time of Jehovah's prophetic utterance at Genesis 3:15 concerning the seed of the woman, this heavenly universal organization has been compared to a faithful wife of a husband and has been spoken of as Jehovah's woman or wife. He, the Creator of this heavenly organization, is its husband, who fathers the seed or offspring it brings forth.[178]

At another place, after Genesis 3:15 has been quoted, it is said,

> By saying that the serpent would be bruised in the head God meant that Satan would be destroyed.   And it would be done by the one whom God would choose.   That one was the Seed of the woman.   The woman was not disobedient Eve, but rather God's heavenly organization of faithful spirit creatures.[179]

The realm of angels, therefore, constitutes Jehovah's woman or the heavenly mother.   The chief Son of this heavenly mother is Jesus Christ, who is the seed of the woman alluded to in Genesis 3:15.[180]

[174] *New Heavens and a New Earth*, p. 20.
[175] *Ibid.*, pp. 26-28.
[176] *Let God Be True*, p. 57.
[177] *New Heavens and a New Earth*, p. 32.
[178] *Ibid.*
[179] *Paradise Lost*, p. 34.   The Hebrew word used for woman in Gen. 3:15 is *'ishshah*.   This word is used throughout the chapter to designate Eve. By what exegetical legerdemain do Jehovah's Witnesses arrive at the astounding conclusion that *'ishshah* in the 15th verse means myriads of angels?
[180] *Ibid.*   It is not easy to determine when, according to the Witnesses, the heavenly woman brought forth Jesus.   It is said at one place that God's woman was childless until A.D. 29, when Jesus was baptized and the Father said, "This is my Son, the beloved" (NWT).   These words, it is stated, mean that the Father now begot Jesus as His spiritual son, and that the Father's woman, the heavenly organization [also called "the Jerusalem above"], had now brought forth the first of her seed (*New*

"Just ten days after Jesus' ascension to heaven, God used his heavenly Zion to bring forth other spiritual children." This happened on the Day of Pentecost, when the holy spirit was poured out, and when many faithful Israelite followers were begotten as spiritual sons.[181] It is further said that the heavenly organization produces all the other members of the anointed class[182]; thus this heavenly organization, and not the earthly church, is the mother of the 144,000. The earthly congregation of anointed ones is, in fact, the visible representation of God's woman on earth.[183]

Next God called into being all the tremendous masses of matter that comprise the material universe; it is this divine act of creation which is referred to in Genesis 1:1.[184] On pages 34 and 35 of *New Heavens and a New Earth* (published in 1953) a guarded and qualified admission is made that the universe may be billions of years old; on page 43 of *Your Will Be Done On Earth* (published in 1958), however, it is stated without qualification that the inanimate material universe is billions of years old. A long period of time is therefore said to have elapsed between this original creation and the beginning of the actual week of creation.[185]

At length, however, the creative week began:

> The time had now come to start getting the earth ready for the animals and humans that would later live on it. So a period began that the Bible calls the "first day." This was not a day of twenty-four hours, but was instead 7,000 years long.[186]

Heavens and a New Earth, p. 153). On p. 201 of this same volume, however, we are told that it was not until Christ's resurrection that the heavenly woman became mother to her first divine, immortal, royal Son. And on pp. 220-21 we are told that God did not open the womb of His woman for the birth of her royal First-born until 1914.

[181] *New Heavens and a New Earth*, p. 203.

[182] *Make Sure of All Things*, p. 75.

[183] *New Heavens and a New Earth*, p. 185. As we shall see when we discuss the fall, some of these angels, under Satan's leadership, rebelled against God and thus became part of the devil's organization.

[184] *Ibid.*, p. 34.

[185] *Paradise Lost*, p. 10. In *What Do the Scriptures Say About "Survival After Death"?* (a booklet published in 1955), p. 58, it is specifically stated that the visible universe is 4½ billion years old. Cf. *You May Survive Armageddon* (1955), p. 21.

[186] *Ibid.* How have the Witnesses arrived at this figure? Since the 7th day, on which God rested from His creative work, is said to be still in progress, and since it is assumed that 6,000 years have elapsed from the time of man's creation to the present, with another 1,000 years to be added to this Sabbath during the coming millennium, it is inferred that the 7th day is

Man was created towards the end of the sixth day, after almost 42,000 years of the creation week had gone by.[187]   The seventh day, on which God rests from creating, is also a 7,000-year day, and is now in progress.

Providence.   Since Jehovah is recognized as Creator and as sovereign, and since all of history is said to be firmly under His control, it may be safely assumed that Jehovah's Witnesses accept the doctrine of divine providence, though the term is not listed in their indexes.   It is said in *Let God Be True* (p. 169) that God has ordained the Sabbath of creation as a means of vindicating Him "as the Creator of what is good and . . . as the Maintainer and Preserver of such good."   This statement implies that God does uphold and preserve His universe.

DOCTRINE OF MAN

THE ORIGINAL STATE OF MAN

The Constitutional Nature of Man.   According to Genesis 2:7 man is a combination of two things: the "dust of the ground" and the "breath of life."   "The combining of these two things (or factors) produced a living soul or creature called *man.*"[188] A study of the way in which the Hebrew word *nephesh* and the Greek word *psuchee* (the Biblical words usually translated *soul*) are used in the Scriptures reveals that these terms are nowhere associated with such words as "immortal, everlasting, eternal, or deathless"; it is concluded, therefore, that the Bible nowhere teaches that the human soul is immortal.[189]   On the contrary, the Bible teaches that the human soul is mortal: witness such passages as Ezekiel 18:4, "the soul that sinneth, it shall die," and Isaiah 53:12, where Christ, who is there predicted, is said to have "poured out his soul unto death."[190]

---

to be 7,000 years long.   From this it is concluded that each of the creation days was of this length (*Let God Be True*, pp. 168, 178).

[187] *Paradise Lost*, p. 18.   It is interesting to note that, though the Witnesses are willing to accept in one area the results of scientific discoveries which have led many in our day to conclude that the universe is very old, they refuse to accept such scientific evidence in another area: namely, as it concerns the age of man.

[188] *Let God Be True*, p. 68.

[189] *Ibid.*, p. 69.

[190] *Ibid.*, pp. 70-71.   On Mt. 10:28, however, which reads: "Do not become fearful of those who kill the body but cannot kill the soul; but rather be in fear of him that can destroy both soul and body in Gehenna" (NWT), their comment is: "the word 'soul' is used [here] as meaning future

At another place *soul* is defined as follows:

> A soul, heavenly or earthly, is a living, sentient (or sense-possessing, conscious, intelligent) creature or person. A soul, heavenly or earthly, consists of a body together with the life principle or life force actuating it.[191]

These statements declare that there can be no soul that exists apart from the body. A man, it is said, *is* a soul; he does not *possess* a soul.[192] Nothing in Scripture, we are told, indicates that Adam after his fall into sin would only *appear to die,* but that his soul would live on forever.[193]

Jehovah's Witnesses therefore oppose the view that man consists of body and soul; they teach that man is a soul which consists of a body together with a life principle which actuates it. They therefore vigorously repudiate the doctrine of the inherent immortality of human souls as the foundation of false religion. It was the devil, in fact, who originated this doctrine, when he said to the woman, "Ye shall not surely die" (Gen. 3:4).[194] On the basis of Ecclesiastes 3:19 and 20 it is further affirmed that men and beasts die alike.[195]

The Image of God. Jehovah's Witnesses declare that man was created in the image of God. This means that man was endowed with God's attributes.

> To man as a creature with God's attributes was granted the privilege of holding dominion over the earth and its forms of life: the birds, fish and animals. Toward these he had the responsibility of exercising the same attributes as his Creator: wisdom in directing the affairs charged to him, justice in dealing

---

life as a soul" (*ibid.,* p. 71). This interpretation, however, is not at all consistent with the view advanced on earlier pages that the soul is mortal and may die. The fact is that in Mt. 10:28 we are plainly told that it is possible to kill the body (*sooma*) without killing the soul (*psuchee*); this passage therefore militates against the Jehovah-Witness contention that the soul in Scripture is always mortal.

[191] *Make Sure of All Things,* p. 349.

[192] *Ibid.*

[193] *Let God Be True,* p. 74.

[194] *Ibid.,* pp. 74-75.

[195] *Ibid.,* p. 75. Note that Jehovah-Witness teaching on the constitutional nature of man is virtually identical with that of Seventh-day Adventism (*The Four Major Cults,* pp. 110-11). It will be recalled that Russell was delivered from his early skepticism by the teachings of an Adventist minister; it would appear, therefore, that he borrowed his view of the soul, which was basically the same as that of present-day Witnesses, from the Adventists (see above, p. 10).

with other creatures of his God, love in unselfishly caring for the earth and its creatures, and power in properly discharging his authority to carry on the right worship of the Universal Sovereign in whose image he was created. — Genesis 1:26-28.[196]

On the basis of Psalm 8:4-8 in the King James version it is implied that man was made a little lower than the angels.[197] Man is, however, superior to the animals, not because he has an immortal soul, but because (1) he is a higher form of creature, and (2) he was originally given dominion over the lower forms of animal life.[198]

MAN IN THE STATE OF SIN

The Fall of Man. God created Adam perfect. In support of this assertion Deuteronomy 32:4 is quoted: "his [God's] work is perfect."[199] This perfect man did not have to die:

> God did not appoint the perfect man to die, but God opened to him the opportunity of everlasting life in human perfection in the Edenic paradise. Only if the perfect man disobeyed would God sentence him to death, and he would cease to exist as a soul.[200]

So then, if man had not sinned, he would not have died. "Had perfect Adam not sinned, it would have been possible for him, though mortal, to live on earth forever and to bequeath life to his children."[201] The words, "though mortal," imply that Adam, even if he had remained sinless, would never have obtained immortality. Yet he would have continued to live on earth forever. How would this have been possible? We get the answer from *Make Sure of All Things*:

> Everlasting life: Life in a perfect organism, fleshly for humans who gain life on earth, spiritual for faithful angels who continue

---

[196] *Let God Be True*, p. 145. No attempt is here made to indicate any distinction between these attributes as they occur in God and in man.

[197] *Ibid.*, p. 67; cf. p. 41.

[198] *Ibid.*, p. 68.

[199] *Ibid.*, p. 117. The application of this passage to the creation of man is, however, of doubtful warrant. A careful reading of the passage, which occurs in the Song of Moses, will reveal that the point of the Hebrew word *tamim* which is here used is that God is beyond reproach in His providential dealings with man.

[200] *This Means Everlasting Life*, p. 32.

[201] *Let God Be True*, p. 74.

to live in heaven. . . . God through his organization protects the life of such individuals for all eternity. Such a person, by his very creation, is dependent upon food, subject to God's laws governing created things.[202]

Adam and Eve, however, did not remain obedient to God; they fell into sin. The Witnesses accept as literal history the story of the fall found in Genesis 3. One of God's good angels, who had been placed in Eden as the overseer of humankind, rebelled against God.[203] Filled with pride, he desired to be equal to God; hence he planned to cause disobedience among God's sons and thus to gather a group of persons who would serve him instead of God.[204] He it was, therefore, who spoke to Eve through the serpent. Beguiled by this rebellious spirit, called the Devil or Satan, Eve first and then Adam ate the fruit of the forbidden tree and thus disobeyed God.[205]

The penalty for this first sin was death — not eternal torment in hell but physical death.[206] Such physical death meant annihilation for man:[207]

> Death did not mean that a soul taken from heaven and encased in Adam's earthly body would escape and return to heaven and live there immortally. No! At death Adam would return to the dust.[208]

God did not, however, immediately execute this death penalty, since Satan had now raised an issue which affected the whole universe, namely, that of the sovereignty of Jehovah.[209] Because Jehovah's sovereignty had to be vindicated, Satan was not destroyed at once; he was given time to bring forth seed, against whom Jehovah would wage war.[210] Adam and Eve were also not

[202] P. 243. Thus Adam would have been sustained everlastingly by the food of his earthly paradise home, and his body would never have become old (*Paradise Lost,* p. 26). Incidentally, we note that the angels, too, would have to be sustained by food (!), since their immortality is denied (*Make Sure of All Things,* p. 247).

[203] *Let God Be True,* pp. 57-58.

[204] *Paradise Lost,* p. 30.

[205] *Ibid.,* pp. 30-32.

[206] *This Means Everlasting Life,* p. 44.

[207] *New Heavens and a New Earth,* p. 84; *Paradise Lost,* p. 28.

[208] *New Heavens and a New Earth,* p. 88.

[209] *This Means Everlasting Life,* p. 42.

[210] *Let God Be True,* pp. 58-59. By the seed of Satan is meant people and spirits who are in league with him and form part of his organization. Cain was the first of Satan's seed (*New Heavens and a New Earth,* p. 91).

put to death at once since they had to be permitted to bring children into the world — so that men might learn about God and so that Jehovah might be vindicated.[211]   When Adam was 930 years old he died.   He did not live out a full thousand-year period, but, since with God one day is as a thousand years, we may say that Adam did die in the same day that he ate of the forbidden fruit. Thus God's word was vindicated: "In the day that thou eatest thereof thou shalt surely die."[212]

> There is not a scrap of evidence that Adam repented.   He was a willful rebel and was beyond repentance, and his sentence is beyond recall. . . .   Adam died and went nowhere but to the dust from which he had been taken.[213]

Original Sin.   What were the results of Adam's sin for his descendants?   Adam brought death not only on himself but on all the race descended from him.[214]   Other results of Adam's fall included inborn sin, imperfection, and disease.[215]   Though we do not have anywhere a clear exposition of what this inborn sin involves, *Let God Be True* speaks of both condemnation and disability.   On page 119 we read about the "inherited condemnation of Adam's descendants," and also of the "inherited disability under which all are born."   On page 117 the results of Adam's sin are expressed as follows: "All his [Adam's] children, we and our ancestors, were born following his sin."

It should be added, however, that Jehovah's Witnesses do not at all have the same understanding of "inborn sin" that is found, say, in the Westminster Confession, the Heidelberg Catechism, or the Augsburg Confession.   According to Romans 8:7 no one who still has the "mind of the flesh" can be subject to the law of God, and according to I John 5:1 no one who is not born again or begotten of God can believe that Jesus is the Christ.   The Witnesses,

---

A large group of angels joined Satan in his rebellion and became demons. It is contended that the fall of the angels is depicted in Genesis 6:1-4, the "sons of God" in this passage being interpreted as angels who "materialized in flesh," and the "daughters of men" being understood to have been human women (*ibid.,* pp. 91-94).

[211] *This Means Everlasting Life,* p. 42.

[212] *The Truth Shall Make You Free,* pp. 111-113.   Though the days of creation are thus said to have been 7,000 years long, and though in prophetic sections of the Bible a day is said to equal a year, the day in which Adam lived is alleged to have been 1,000 years long!

[213] *Ibid.,* p. 113.

[214] *New Heavens and a New Earth,* p. 89.

[215] *Religion for Mankind,* p. 63.

however, do not agree with this clear teaching of Scripture. They declare that only the 144,000 have been and will be born again or begotten of God. Since this congregation of 144,000 began to be gathered after Pentecost,[216] no one could have been regenerated before Pentecost. Yet many served God faithfully in Old Testament times, according to them, and will therefore be raised as other sheep during the millennium. Furthermore, since Pentecost, and particularly since 1931 (they are rather vague on the period between Pentecost and 1931), the vast majority of Jehovah's Witnesses have been, and are still, other sheep. These other sheep however, *cannot be born again.* Yet they are said to be able to exercise true faith,[217] to be faithful to Jehovah,[218] to belong to "obedient mankind,"[219] and to dedicate themselves to do God's will.[220] The Witnesses, therefore, teach that a person can believe and be faithful to Jehovah without having been born again!

I conclude that, though Jehovah's Witnesses appear to teach an inherited disability on account of Adam's sin, their theology belies this assertion. For a "disability" which enables unregenerate man to have true faith, to dedicate his life to God, and to remain faithful to Jehovah is no disability at all!

DOCTRINE OF CHRIST

THE PERSON OF CHRIST

The Prehuman State. In order to understand Jehovah-Witness teaching on the person of Christ, we shall have to distinguish between a prehuman, a human, and a posthuman state. To begin with the prehuman state, Christ, it is said, was the first creature of Jehovah.[221] During this prehuman state, which lasted from the time of the Son's creation to the time when he was born of Mary, Christ was the Logos or Word of the Father. This does not mean, however, that he was equal to the Father; the title Logos only implies that the Son was the spokesman for God the Father to other creatures that were called into being after him.[222] Thus the

216 *New Heavens and a New Earth,* p. 203.
217 *This Means Everlasting Life,* p. 295.
218 *Let God Be True,* p. 231.
219 *New Heavens and a New Earth,* p. 336.
220 *Let God Be True,* p. 298.
221 See above, p. 47.
222 *Let God Be True,* p. 33; *The Truth Shall Make You Free,* p. 44.

Son was the Chief Executive Officer of Jehovah and, as such, superior to all other creatures.[223]

Jehovah's Witnesses insist, however, that neither in this state nor in any subsequent state is the Son equal to Jehovah. As a matter of fact, during his prehuman state the Son was really an angel. Previous to the Son's coming to earth as a man he was not known in heaven as Jesus Christ, but as Michael; when we read in Jude 9 about Michael the archangel, we are to understand this expression as a designation of Jesus Christ in his prehuman state.[224] Between Christ in his prehuman state and the angels, therefore, there is a difference only of degree but not of kind; it will be recalled that, according to the Witnesses, the angels are higher than man, but only creatures.

Yet, though the Son was only a creature during his pre-human state, Jehovah's Witnesses insist that he was at that time some kind of god. On the basis of their translation of John 1:1 ("In [the] beginning the Word was, and the Word was with God, and the Word was a god," NWT), they call the Word "a god,"[225] or say that he had "a godly quality."[226] The Witnesses interpret the so-called *kenosis* passage of Philippians 2:5-8 as meaning that the Son "did not follow the course of the Devil and plot and scheme to make himself like or equal to the Most High God and to rob God or usurp God's place."[227] To support this interpretation they appeal to their own renderings of the passage in the *New World Translation* and in the *Emphatic Diaglott*.[228]

While he was in this prehuman state, the Son, in common with the other angels, did not possess immortality. Later, however, Jehovah "opened up to his Son the opportunity to gain immortality."[229]

The Human State. The following quotation from a recent book sets forth in some detail the Jehovah-Witness view of the concep-

---

[223] *The Truth Shall Make You Free*, p. 44.

[224] *New Heavens and a New Earth*, pp. 28-30. These pages also contain the Scriptural evidence adduced to prove this point.

[225] *Let God Be True*, p. 34.

[226] *The Word — Who Is He?* (booklet pub. in 1962), p. 56.

[227] *Let God Be True*, pp. 34-35.

[228] *Ibid.*, pp. 32, 35. These passages, and others adduced by Jehovah's Witnesses to substantiate their view of the person of Christ, will be dealt with more fully in the Appendix.

[229] *The Truth Shall Make You Free*, p. 44. Cf. above, n. 202, and see discussion of Christ's posthuman state.

tion, birth, and nature of Jesus Christ while he was on earth:

> To become born of Mary the heavenly Son had to lay aside
> all his heavenly glory and position. At God's due time for
> his only-begotten Son to become a man, Jehovah took the
> perfect life of his only-begotten Son and transferred it from
> heaven to the egg cell in the womb of the unmarried girl
> Mary. God, by his almighty power, was able to take the
> personality of his only-begotten Son, his life pattern, and put
> this personality within the powers of the tiny bundle of live
> energy that he placed into the womb of Mary. Thus God's Son
> was conceived or given a start as a human creature. It was
> a miracle. Under Jehovah's holy power the child Jesus, con-
> ceived in this way, grew in Mary's womb to the point of birth.
> Thus the child Jesus was born with all the marvelous qualities
> of righteousness in him just as a child inherits qualities from
> his father. Having a perfect Father as his life source, Jesus
> did not inherit imperfection from his imperfect mother Mary.[230]

From these paragraphs it is clear that the Witnesses do not
deny the virgin birth of Christ, as has recently been alleged.[231] Note
that what is said to have been transferred from heaven to Mary's
womb was the "life," the "personality," or the "life pattern" of the
Son of God, who, it will be recalled, was never equal to Jehovah
but was only a created angel. What happened when Jesus was
born, therefore, was not the incarnation of God. ". . . Jesus' birth
on earth was not an incarnation."[232] Christ was therefore not God
in the flesh.

But now the question arises: Is there real continuity between
the Son of God in his prehuman and his human state? Was the
child born of Mary really the same individual who existed previously in heaven as the Archangel Michael? To this question it is

---

[230] *Paradise Lost*, p. 127. Cf. *Let God Be True*, p. 36; *The Kingdom is at
Hand*, p. 49; *New Heavens and a New Earth*, pp. 150, 153. On the last-
named page the work of the spirit in overshadowing Mary is also mentioned.

[231] John H. Gerstner, *The Theology of the Major Sects*, p. 36.

[232] *Religion for Mankind*, p. 231. It is quite revealing to note what the
Jehovah-Witness conception of incarnation is: "Moreover, if a mere incarnation of the Son of God had been intended, then it would not have
been necessary for him to have his life transferred to an embryo in the
virgin's womb and to be developed there and finally born as a helpless infant.
He could still have remained a spirit person and materialized a fully developed fleshly body and clothed himself with it, just as . . . the angel
Gabriel did when appearing visibly to Mary" (*The Truth Shall Make You
Free*, p. 245). Actually, however, what is here described is not an incarnation but a temporary assumption of a body for the purpose of bringing
a message.

difficult to give an unambiguous answer. On the one hand, Jehovah's Witnesses frequently speak of "Christ's prehuman existence,"[233] say that the angel Michael was actually Jesus Christ in his prehuman spirit form,[234] and assert that it was God's only-begotten Son who became a man.[235] Other passages from their writings, however, imply that there was no real continuity between Michael and the man Jesus Christ:

> That the Son of God born on earth was no mighty spirit person clothing himself with a baby's fleshly form and pretending to be absolutely ignorant like a newborn infant is proved by the scripture (Philippians 2:5-8), which shows he laid aside completely his spirit existence. . . .[236]
>
> By this miracle [the virgin birth] he was born a man (Philippians 2:7 . . .). He was not a spirit-human hybrid, a man and at the same time a spirit person. He was not clothed upon with flesh over an invisible spirit person, but he WAS flesh.[237]

If Christ, however, was not a spirit person during his human state, but only a man, was not his birth the birth of a new individual, rather than a transfer of a heavenly life to the womb of Mary? If Christ completely laid aside his previous spirit existence, how could he still be the individual who had lived in that spirit existence? The thrust of the above two quotations is clearly this: when Christ was born of Mary, he stopped being a spirit person and became a man — nothing more than a man.

One point has become very clear: Jehovah's Witnesses do not believe that Christ had (or has) two natures. While on earth Christ had only one nature: the nature of a man. Since previous to his birth from Mary, the Son of God is said to have had a spirit nature, of which he divested himself at the time he came to earth, we must conclude, according to Watchtower teaching, that the Christ who was born in Bethlehem is not the same individual who existed previously as the Archangel Michael.[238]

---

[233] *Let God Be True*, p. 34; *New Heavens and a New Earth*, p. 28; *The Word — Who Is He*, p. 38.

[234] *New Heavens and a New Earth*, p. 27; cf. p. 30.

[235] *Paradise Lost*, p. 127.

[236] *The Truth Shall Make You Free*, p. 246.

[237] *Religion for Mankind*, p. 231.

[238] It is thus evident that Jehovah's Witnesses reject Chalcedon as well as Nicaea. The Witnesses might counter the above argumentation by saying that since the *life* of the heavenly being was transferred to Mary's womb there is some continuity after all. In reply I would say: But the life which was transferred was not the life of a spirit person. Where, then, is the

It should further be added that Christ was born as "a perfect human creature."[239] The reason for this is that Christ had to be the absolute equivalent of the perfect man Adam in Eden. Since, according to Deuteronomy 19:21, God had said "Soul (*nephesh*) will be for soul, eye for eye, tooth for tooth . . ." (NWT), it is obvious that another perfect man must be sacrificed to undo the harm wrought by Adam's fall.[240] "Hence as the human life privileges had been forfeited for the human race by its perfect father Adam, through sin, those life privileges had to be repurchased by the sacrifice of a perfect human life like Jesus'."[241]

Before we go on to consider Christ's posthuman state, something should be said about the significance of Christ's baptism since this will shed light on the Witnesses' view of his person. When Jesus was baptized, there came a voice from heaven saying, "This is my son, the beloved, whom I have approved" (Mt. 3:17, NWT). This meant that "as God by his spirit overshadowing Mary transferred his Son's life from heaven to her womb, now God by that same spirit begot Jesus to become his spiritual son."[242] The coming down of the spirit upon Christ in the form of a dove represented the fact that Christ was now anointed with God's spirit, thus becoming Jehovah's High Priest.[243] By this act Christ became " 'a new creation' with spirit life in the invisible heavens in view."[244] By this act Christ also became God's Anointed One or Christ — the Heir of the heavenly Kingdom.[245]

According to the above statements Christ was not Jehovah's High Priest, nor the Messiah, nor the Heir of the heavenly Kingdom until he had been baptized! More serious still, these state-

---

continuity? Since Jehovah's Witnesses do not teach the pre-existence of man, we must conclude that the life of Jesus as a man began with his miraculous conception. But this was a human life, not an angelic life.

[239] *New Heavens and a New Earth*, p. 151.

[240] *Ibid.*, pp. 151-52.

[241] *Ibid.*, p. 152.

[242] *Ibid.*, p. 153. At another place it is said that at this time God "begot Jesus to be his spiritual Son once more instead of a human Son" (*Let God Be True*, p. 38). The words "once more" imply that the Son was a spiritual Son during his prehuman state, but that he ceased being a spiritual Son when he was conceived and born of Mary. This statement thus underscores the discontinuity that exists between the first and second states of Christ's existence.

[243] *New Heavens and a New Earth*, p. 153.

[244] *Your Will Be Done*, p. 138. It is implied that if Christ had not been thus spirit-begotten, he would not have been entitled to enjoy spirit life in heaven when his earthly life was over.

[245] *Ibid.*

ments clearly avow that Christ was not a spiritual or spirit-begotten Son of God until his baptism. Since the members of the anointed class must also become spiritual sons,[246] and be begotten by God's spirit,[247] it is obvious that there is a very close analogy between Christ and the members of the anointed class. Since Christ while on earth was not God, and not a spirit person, but only a man (though a sinless man), we may say that the difference between Christ and the 144,000 is not one of kind but only one of degree.

The Posthuman State. Jehovah God raised Christ from the dead, "not as a human Son, but as a mighty immortal spirit Son. . . ."[248] The physical resurrection of Jesus Christ is therefore denied; Christ was raised not with the same body which he had before, but as a "spirit Son, no longer flesh.[249] The reasoning behind this teaching is as follows: In order to atone for the sin of Adam, Christ had to sacrifice his human body. This means that he had to renounce it permanently and could not get it back again. Therefore God raised him as a spirit Son.[250] The Scripture passage usually cited to substantiate this view is I Peter 3:18, "Being put to death in the flesh, but being made alive in the spirit" (NWT).

What happened to the body of Christ? ". . . Jehovah God disposed of that body in his own way, just as he disposed of the body of Moses, who was a type of Christ Jesus; but no one knows how."[251] Rutherford had surmised that the Lord may have preserved it somewhere to exhibit to the people in the millennial age.[252]

At another place it is stated that Christ was raised not with a body of flesh, but "in a spirit body."[253] This "spirit body," however, which Christ had after his resurrection, was not a visible body. How, then, did Christ reveal himself to his disciples after his resurrection? "By materializing fleshly bodies on the occasions

[246] *Let God Be True,* p. 300.
[247] *This Means Everlasting Life,* p. 121.
[248] *Let God Be True,* p. 40.
[249] *Religion for Mankind,* p. 259; cf. *Make Sure of All Things,* p. 314.
[250] *Religion for Mankind,* p. 259.
[251] *The Truth Shall Make You Free,* p. 264.
[252] *The Harp of God,* 1928, p. 173. If, however, it had to be demonstrated that Christ had permanently renounced his body, why was his body not left in the tomb?
[253] *The Truth Shall Make You Free,* p. 264. Cf. *Make Sure of All Things,* p. 349, where we read that a heavenly soul, as well as an earthly soul, consists of "a body together with the life principle or life force actuating it."

of his appearances," each such body being different from the others.[254]   These were temporary materializations, comparable to those in which angels had occasionally appeared to men.[255]

At the time of his resurrection Christ was given immortality as a reward for his faithful course on earth; he was, in fact, the first creature to receive this gift.[256]   God now exalted his Son to be higher than he was before he lived and died as a man, and made him to be Head under Jehovah of God's capital organization over the universe.[257]   The Son now resumed the name Michael, "to tie him with his prehuman existence."[258]

Since, according to Watchtower teaching, there is no such thing as an immaterial soul which persists after death, and since Christ's material body was not raised, we are forced to conclude that Christ was actually annihilated when he died. While on earth Christ was only a man, with a nature which was only human; this human nature, however, was sacrificed on the cross[259] so completely that he could not get it back again. It will not do to say that Christ sacrificed only his human body and not his human soul, since the Witnesses recognize no human soul which survives the body. The life which Christ now enjoys is not human life, nor the life of a divine Person with a human nature, but angelic life — life as a spirit-creature called Michael. It is obvious, therefore, that Christ after his resurrection is for the Witnesses not in any sense human, or a being with a human nature. Thus there is no real continuity, either, between the second and the third state of Christ's existence. For this reason Jehovah's Witnesses cannot really speak of the exaltation of Christ, since the individual who is exalted is not the same being as the individual who was humiliated.

I conclude that what the three states of Christ's existence in

---

[254] *The Truth Shall Make You Free*, pp. 265-67.
[255] *Let God Be True*, p. 40.
[256] *Ibid.*, p. 74.
[257] *Ibid.*, p. 40.
[258] *Your Will Be Done*, p. 316.
[259] Jehovah's Witnesses prefer to speak of "torture stake" instead of "cross," since they believe that Jesus was put to death on a simple upright stake, without a crossbar; their NWT, therefore, also renders the Greek verb *stauro-oo* (crucify) as "impale."   H. J. Spier, in his *De Jehovah's Getuigen en de Bijbel* (Kampen: Kok, 1961), pp. 132-33, has shown the untenability of this interpretation. See also Alfred Edersheim, *Life and Times of Jesus the Messiah* (New York: Longmans, Green, & Co., 1901), II, 584-85; and J. D. Douglas, ed., *The New Bible Dictionary* (Eerdmans, 1962), p. 279.

Watchtower theology really amount to is this: angel — man — angel, with no real continuity between the three. A little reflection will reveal how devastating this view is of the Christology of the Scriptures. The individual who laid down his life at Calvary was not the individual who existed previously in heaven and was God's agent in creation; the individual who is now ruling over his heavenly Kingdom is not the individual who died on the cross for us. Really, Jehovah's Witnesses have three Christs, none of whom is equal to Jehovah and none of whom is the Christ of the Scriptures.

THE WORK OF CHRIST

The Atonement. As we have seen, because of Adam's sin all men have inherited physical death and inborn sin. Jesus Christ, the Witnesses teach, made atonement for us and thus removed for believers the results of Adam's sin. The word *atonement,* it is said, is drawn from the expression *at one,* and means that what makes satisfaction for another thing which has been forfeited must be "at one" with that other thing, that is, must be exactly equivalent to it.[260] When applied to the work of Christ, atonement means that "the human life that Jesus Christ laid down in sacrifice must be exactly equal to that life which Adam forfeited for all his offspring; it must be a perfect human life, no more, no less."[261]

This human life which Jesus sacrificed for his people is called a *ransom.* A ransom is defined as "that which buys back, loosens or releases . . . more especially, releasing from inherited sin and from prospects of eternal death as a result of sin."[262] God provided through Christ a redemptive price whereby "those of men who have faith in God's provision may come into harmony with him and, serving him faithfully, they may receive the gift of life, being freed from inherited sin and from eternal death as a result of sin."[263]

Since what was lost in Adam was perfect human life with its rights and earthly prospects, what is redeemed or bought back is

[260] *You May Survive Armageddon,* pp. 38-39. Webster's *New Collegiate Dictionary,* 1956 ed., agrees that *atone* comes from *at one,* but defines *at one* in this sense as meaning "in concord or friendship" (p. 55). It would appear that the Jehovah-Witness derivation of this word is not accurate.
[261] *You May Survive Armageddon,* p. 39.
[262] *Make Sure of All Things,* pp. 293-94.
[263] *Let God Be True,* p. 113. By "eternal death" in this quotation is meant annihilation.

also perfect human life with its rights and earthly prospects.[264]
This is exactly what Jesus laid down in death: a perfect human
life, with all its rights and earthly prospects. Since this human life
was not given back to Jesus, this sacrificed human life remained
effective,

> a thing of value with purchasing power, hence with ransoming
> or redemptive power. The value of the perfect human life was
> now available for use on behalf of faithful men needing to be
> ransomed thereby.[265]

It is expressly denied that the atonement of Christ was a satisfaction of divine justice:

> Justice was satisfied in mankind's suffering death, the just
> penalty of sin. So the ransom is an expression of God's mercy,
> his undeserved kindness toward mankind.[266]

This statement must be understood against the background of Jehovah-Witness teaching that the penalty for Adam's sin was not
eternal torment in hell but physical death which was to be followed
by annihilation. The purpose of Christ's death, then, was to
rescue men from the annihilation in which they would otherwise
have remained after death. The question, however, must now be
raised: what happens to the justice of God when people are raised
from the dead? Since God's justice required man's death *and
annihilation,* how can it be said that the justice of God is satisfied
by the death of people who are later raised again? If Christ did
not in any sense satisfy God's justice by his atoning work, we shall
have to conclude that, for Jehovah's Witnesses, the justice of God
is so weak that He simply relaxes its demands in the case of those
who come to believe in Christ.

What is said about Christ's removal of the curse, however, is not
consistent with the above. It is taught that Christ had to hang on
the "stake" as an accursed one in order to deliver the Jews from
the curse of the law which rested upon them for their transgres-
sions, particularly for their rejection of God's Messiah.[267] At another place we are told that Christ died not just for the curse on
the Jews, but for the "condemnation of sin on all mankind."[268] If
this is so, there must be a sense in which Christ's death did satisfy

---

[264] *Ibid.,* p. 114.
[265] *Ibid.,* p. 116.
[266] *Ibid.,* p. 115. The implication is that the ransom was an expression
of God's mercy but not in any sense an expression of God's justice.
[267] *This Means Everlasting Life,* pp. 109-10; *Paradise Lost,* p. 144.
[268] *Religion for Mankind,* p. 148.

God's justice or appease God's wrath. For how otherwise could God remove the curse of the law or the condemnation of sin?

The Extent of the Atonement. For whom did Christ make this atonement? Not for everyone. It is specifically stated that Adam is not included among those ransomed.[269] Those who remain eternally dead and are thus permanently annihilated are also said not to have been ransomed.[270] It is further stated that Christ laid down his life for the other sheep as well as for the bride class,[271] for non-Jews as well as for Jews,[272] for all the "worthy ones of Adam's children,"[273] and for all the believers of Adam's family.[274] This ransom provides the basis for the "resurrection of the dead who are in God's memory and their eventual gaining of life."[275] The ransom, in fact, extends its benefits even to those who "practiced vile things" on earth, but who will be raised during the millennium and will then be given the opportunity of responding to the gospel.[276]

As we reflect upon this view of the atonement, we note how far it falls short of Biblical doctrine. First, the sacrifice brought by Christ, for the Witnesses, was not of infinite value since it was the sacrifice of a mere human life. There is no hint in their teachings of the thought expressed in Anselm's *Cur Deus Homo* that the "price paid to God for the sin of man [must] be something greater than all the universe besides God,"[277] and that therefore the one who pays this price must in his own person be God.

---

[269] *Let God Be True*, p. 119. The reason here given is: "Because he was a willful sinner, was justly sentenced to death, and died deservedly, and God would not reverse his just judgment and give Adam life." Apparently the Witnesses exclude the possibility that Adam may have repented of his sin, and may have exercised faith in the promise of salvation recorded in Gen. 3:15 (see above, n. 213).

[270] *Make Sure of All Things*, p. 296.

[271] *You May Survive Armageddon*, p. 230.

[272] *Let God Be True*, p. 119.

[273] *Paradise Lost*, p. 143.

[274] *Let God Be True*, p. 119.

[275] *Ibid.*, p. 120.

[276] *Ibid.*, p. 280. As will be seen when we discuss the doctrine of salvation and the doctrine of the last things, however, what really determines the salvation of those to whom Christ's ransom is to be applied is not the merits of Christ but the works of men. Note, e.g., the following statement: ". . . the course of an individual determines whether he will ultimately receive benefit from the ransom sacrifice of Christ or not" (*ibid.*, p. 120).

[277] Translated by Sidney Deane (La Salle: Open Court, 1959), p. 244 (Book II, Chap. 6). Scripture proof for the full deity of the Saviour will be given in the Appendix. Suffice it here to say that Phil. 2:5-8, when properly interpreted, teaches that the one who died on the cross was fully God.

It should further be pointed out that, though Jehovah's Witnesses repeatedly say that God sent His Son Christ Jesus to earth to provide this ransom,[278] and that the one who did the ransoming work was therefore the same individual who was previously with God in heaven,[279] their teachings about the person of Christ do not warrant this conclusion. For, as has been pointed out, there is no real continuity between Christ as he appeared in the flesh and the previously existing Archangel Michael.[280] For the Witnesses, therefore, God did not really send his only-begotten Son (even if one understands this term as designating the created Logos) into the world to ransom man from his sins. Rather, He caused a sinless man to be miraculously conceived by Mary; this man was not even a "spirit-begotten son of God" at birth, but only a human son. He was different from other men only in two respects: (1) he had been born of a virgin, and (2) he lived a perfect life. But Jehovah's Witnesses cannot consistently maintain that the individual whom they call Jesus Christ was the same individual who had existed previously with God as His only-begotten Son and who had been God's agent in creation.

At this point the question cannot be suppressed: Why should the sacrificed life of Jesus Christ have so much value that it can serve to ransom millions of people from annihilation? It was a perfect human life which was sacrificed, to be sure; we must not minimize this point. But it was the perfect human life of someone who was *only a man.* Could the life of a mere man, offered in sacrifice, serve to purchase a multitude which no man can number?[281]

DOCTRINE OF SALVATION

Who will benefit from the ransom of Christ? At this point the anti-Reformation character of Watchtower teachings becomes very clear: "By willingly laying down his human life he [Christ] could use its right to buy back the worthy ones of Adam's children."[282] It is, however, impossible to discuss Jehovah-Witness soteriology without distinguishing between the "anointed class" and the "other sheep," since the way of salvation is not the same for both:

[278] *Let God Be True,* p. 113.
[279] *Ibid.,* p. 115.
[280] See above, pp. 62-63.
[281] What the Witnesses teach about the work of Christ (that is, the spirit creature who "arose" from Jesus' grave) since his "resurrection" will be treated under the Doctrine of the Last Things.
[282] *Paradise Lost,* p. 143. Cf. n. 276 above.

All who by reason of faith in Jehovah God and in Christ Jesus dedicate themselves to do God's will and then faithfully carry out their dedication will be rewarded with everlasting life (Romans 6:23). However, that life will not be the same for all. The Bible plainly shows that some of these, that is, 144,000, will share in heavenly glory with Christ Jesus, while the others will enjoy the blessings of life down here on earth (Revelation 14:1, 3; Micah 4:1-5).[283]

The Anointed Class. Since the way of salvation is more elaborate and complex for the anointed class than it is for the other sheep, we shall first look at the doctrine of salvation as it applies to the anointed class or 144,000. How do they obtain salvation? They must first believe and repent. Faith is defined as follows:

Faith means that by reason of Bible knowledge one has a firm assurance that God exists and that he will reward those who earnestly seek him, and that the Bible is his truth and man's sure guide. It further means to accept Jesus not only as a Teacher and Example but also as one's Savior and Ransomer. Such faith causes one to be converted or turned, to change his course of action.[284]

This faith includes not only knowledge of the message of the Bible but also acceptance of Christ, followed by a change of life.[285]

Repentance is also required. In *Make Sure of All Things* repentance is thus defined: "Recognition and admission of a wrong condition or course of action, and a sincere sorrow with determination, motivated by a wholehearted desire to conform to right principles, to turn forever from such wrong course and take a course in harmony with God's will" (p. 307). In the light of what was said about faith, it is evident that repentance is a fruit of true faith.

True faith and true repentance thus require that one should "give up one's selfish course and dedicate oneself to do God's will, just as Jesus did."[286] Dedication, which is required of all who want to serve God, is defined as follows:

[283] *Let God Be True,* p. 298.
[284] *Ibid.,* pp. 295-96.
[285] It is said in *Make Sure of All Things,* p. 120, that faith is a gift from God. On the other hand, however, after the authors of *Paradise Lost* have described faith, repentance, and dedication, they go on to say, "This much the individual can do. The rest [meaning the other steps necessary for becoming a member of the anointed class, here called "the spiritual nation"] depends upon God" (p. 152).
[286] *Let God Be True,* p. 296.

> Christian dedication is the act of a person in setting himself apart by solemn agreement, unreservedly and unconditionally, to do the will of Jehovah God through Christ Jesus, as that will is set forth in the Bible, being made plain by God's holy spirit. It means one must live a holy life, separate from this world, and serve God henceforth to eternity.[287]

Since Jesus publicly confessed his dedication to do his Father's will by being baptized, everyone who has similarly agreed to do God's will should be baptized, as a symbol of his dedication. This baptism, however, must be by immersion.[288]

In order to enter into the heavenly glory for which they are destined, the members of the anointed class "must undergo the sacrifice of all human life right and hopes, even as Jesus did."[289] Since, however, these people are sinners, they do not have either the right to life or an acceptable body to offer as a sacrifice. Hence they must first be justified or declared righteous before they can undergo the sacrifice of human life-right and hopes.[290]

When and how does this justification occur? It is not easy to answer the first of these two questions since it is said that God declares such a person righteous "because of his faith in Christ's blood."[291] Actually, these individuals already exercised faith in Christ's blood before their baptism since faith is a prerequisite for baptism.[292] It appears, however, that this justification does not take place until after one has been baptized.[293] As far as the "how" of this justification is concerned, we read in *Let God Be True*:

> Christ Jesus then [after one has exercised faith and has dedicated himself to God] acts as an advocate, covering the sins of such a dedicated one by the merit of his sacrifice. The dedicated one is now in position to be justified or declared righteous by God, and thus he has access to God through Christ Jesus. He has an acceptable body and the right to perfect life on earth, and all this can be presented for sacrifice with Christ Jesus.[294]

[287] *Make Sure of All Things*, p. 91.
[288] *Let God Be True*, pp. 296-98.
[289] *Ibid.*, p. 299.
[290] *Ibid.*
[291] *Paradise Lost*, p. 152.
[292] *Ibid.*
[293] *Ibid.* Cf. *Let God Be True*, p. 299.
[294] P. 299. See also *Paradise Lost*, p. 152. What is puzzling, however, is that, though this justification is described in these two places as an act in which God declares these people righteous, in *New Heavens and a New Earth*, p. 167, we read, "For their [the members of the anointed class] prov-

It is to be noted that the justification of the 144,000 is solely for the purpose of enabling them to sacrifice their right to life on earth so that they can share the life of Christ in heaven.[295]

What is the next step? "God now choosing them [the 144,000], he accepts the High Priest's sacrifice of the dedicated ones and causes his active force or holy spirit to act upon them so as to bring them forth as spiritual sons with the hope of life in the heavens and he [God] acknowledges them as his sons."[296] So the members of the anointed class are now brought forth as spiritual sons of God. At this time God gives to such persons his holy spirit;[297] they now also have "prospects and hopes for spirit life by resurrection to heaven."[298]

These persons now become members of Christ's body, and thus receive of his anointing.[299] God now consecrates them or sets them apart for a holy work;[300] this anointing or consecration means that they are made kings and priests of God, in which double capacity they will rule, together with Christ, over the rest of mankind.[301] The holy spirit is for the anointed ones a pledge guaranteeing their heavenly inheritance.[302]

These anointed ones do not yet have immortality at this time, but have a hope of it set before them and therefore seek it as a prize. "To gain that incorruptible prize they must be loyal to God even at the cost of their human lives."[303]

> Before such members of Christ's body can receive their heavenly inheritance they must be set apart more and more from this world and to the holy service of Jehovah God, demonstrat-

---

ing faithful imitators of his Son to the close of their earthly life, making their calling and their being chosen certain, Jehovah God will pronounce them righteous. . . ." Is there a difference between "declaring righteous" and "pronouncing righteous"? If so, the latter occurs at the close of the earthly life of the 144,000, and is based not on faith, but on works. If not, Jehovah's Witnesses are not consistent on this point.

[295] Cf. *This Means Everlasting Life*, pp. 120-21.

[296] *Let God Be True*, pp. 299-300. It will be remembered that Christ was also begotten or brought forth as a spiritual son of God at the time of his baptism.

[297] *Paradise Lost*, p. 152.

[298] *Make Sure of All Things*, p. 48. This is the reason, I presume, why the other sheep do not need to be born again — they have no prospects of spirit life in heaven.

[299] *Let God Be True*, p. 300.

[300] *Paradise Lost*, p. 152.

[301] *New Heavens and a New Earth*, p. 307; *Paradise Lost*, p. 153.

[302] *Let God Be True*, p. 300.

[303] *This Means Everlasting Life*, p. 121.

ing their dependability by carrying out their dedication faithfully until death. This work of setting them apart the Scriptures speak of as "sanctification". . . .[304]

The anointed ones, therefore, are also sanctified; in this process both the Creator and the dedicated ones have a part.[305]

The anointed ones must preach the good news of Christ's Kingdom. If they maintain their integrity until death, they will receive immortality. God is now using these consecrated members of Christ's body to direct the work of proclaiming his Name and Kingdom. The earthly remnant of his body is known as the "faithful and discreet slave";[306] it is the task of this remnant to provide spiritual food for those who hunger and thirst after truth.[307]

As we reflect on the way of salvation for the 144,000, we remember what was said in *Paradise Lost,* p. 152, about the earlier stages of this process: "This much the individual can do. The rest depends upon God." Jehovah's Witnesses teach that the selection of the 144,000 is a sovereign act on God's part. This selection, however, is made on the basis of their having met the requirements for membership in this class.[308] One is chosen to belong to this group, therefore, on the basis of his worthiness. We must remember, too, that the first steps in the process which leads to salvation for this class are faith, repentance, and dedication to Christ — steps which these individuals themselves must take. It is only after they have taken these steps that God justifies, regenerates, and sanctifies them. It should further be noted that much emphasis is laid on continued faithfulness to God. These people must "demonstrate their dependability by carrying out their dedication faithfully until death."[309] If they turn back from this dedication, such turning back "would mark them as agreement-breakers, worthy of death, annihilation."[310] As a matter of fact, salvation for the Witnesses is not something which one receives when he

[304] *Let God Be True,* p. 301.
[305] *Ibid.* Strange to say, however, the passage quoted to support this point is Lev. 20:7, 8. But the anointed class (who are the only ones that will be sanctified in this sense) did not begin to be gathered until Pentecost! (see above, p. 54).
[306] *Let God Be True,* pp. 302-303. By earthly remnant is meant the members of the anointed class who are still left on earth at any one time.
[307] *Ibid.,* p. 132.
[308] See above, p. 51.
[309] *Let God Be true,* p. 301.
[310] *Ibid.,* pp. 302-3.

becomes a Christian, but something which is not fully attained until one's earthly course is finished.[311]

Hence, though Jehovah's Witnesses claim that salvation is of grace, and that all credit for salvation belongs to Jehovah,[312] we conclude that in Watchtower theology it is not really God's sovereign grace that saves even the 144,000, but rather man who saves himself by grasping the ransom, by showing himself worthy of being selected as a member of the anointed class, and by carrying out his dedication to Jehovah faithfully until death. Another point should here be noted. What Christ earned by his ranson, as we have seen, was a perfect human life with its rights and earthly prospects. When the anointed ones are justified, they receive this right to perfect life on earth. This right, however, they now proceed to sacrifice, as Jesus had done before them; by so doing they obtain the right to share heavenly life with Christ after death.[313] Thus they obtain the right to heavenly life, not through Christ's sacrifice (since he earned only the right to perfect life on earth), but through their own sacrifice of their earthly prospects in the Paradise of the New World. It is therefore literally true that these 144,000 earn their own way to heaven!

The Other Sheep. How do the other sheep obtain salvation? They, too, need to have faith in Jehovah and in Jesus Christ; they, too, must dedicate themselves to do God's will and must faithfully carry out their dedication[314]; they, too, must be baptized by immersion as a symbol of their dedication.[315]

Note, however, the following differences between the way of salvation for the other sheep and for the anointed class:

(1) The other sheep do not need to sacrifice the prospect of perfect human life in the coming earthly Paradise.[316]

(2) Hence God does not need to justify them — at least not during their present existence.[317]

---

[311] *Make Sure of All Things,* p. 332.
[312] *Ibid.,* p. 336.
[313] *Let God Be True,* pp. 299-300. Cf. *This Means Everlasting Life,* p. 120; *New Heavens and a New Earth,* p. 309.
[314] *Let God Be True,* p. 298.
[315] *Make Sure of All Things,* p. 30.
[316] *New Heavens and a New Earth,* p. 309.
[317] The reason for the qualification is this: the Witnesses teach that there will be a justification of the other sheep at the end of the millennium. After describing how the other sheep who have been given new bodies during the millennium resist Satan's final attempt to draw them away from God, the authors of *You May Survive Armageddon* say: "God will be

(3) God therefore does not need to regenerate the other sheep; in fact, they cannot be born again.[318]

(4) Neither does God need to consecrate or anoint them to be kings and priests.[319]

(5) Neither does God need to sanctify them.[320]

Since the vast majority of Jehovah's Witnesses today belong to the other sheep, and since the vast majority of those who will be resurrected and saved during the millennium will belong to the other sheep as well, I conclude that, according to Watchtower teaching, most of those who are to be saved will attain this salvation without being regenerated, justified (in the Christian sense), anointed to office, and sanctified (in the Christian sense). This means that, without having their sinful natures renewed, this "great crowd" will be able to have faith in Christ, to dedicate their lives wholly to him, and to remain faithful to the end! This means that the vast majority of believers are not priests or kings — Jehovah's Witnesses thus deny the universal priesthood of believers, one of the basic truths of the Protestant Reformation. This means, too, that the vast majority of believers are not justified by faith but must earn their justification by their "unbreakable steadfastness" during the millennium — thus the Witnesses repudiate the so-called material principle of the Reformation: justification by faith. Looking at all this, one is forced to the conclusion that, in this theological system, man is saved not primarily

---

vindicated as true by their unbreakable steadfastness and he will judge them worthy of the right to everlasting life in the earthly paradise. He will accordingly justify them [the other sheep], and the names of these unchangeably righteous ones will be 'written in the book of life'" (p. 360; cf. *New Heavens and a New Earth*, pp. 355-56; *This Means Everlasting Life*, p. 304). This type of "justification," however, is something quite different from that which the 144,000 are said to receive when they believe. For the justification of the 144,000 is said to be by faith, whereas that of the other sheep is a justification earned by their works.

[318] *Make Sure of All Things*, pp. 48-49. See, e.g., the discussion in *This Means Everlasting Life*, pp. 120-21, which makes it quite clear that only those destined for heavenly life will be begotten by God's spirit.

[319] *Make Sure of All Things*, p. 91: "Consecration . . . . applies only to Christ and the anointed, spirit-begotten members of his body."

[320] *You May Survive Armageddon*, p. 252. Again we note the tendency to use theological terms in a variety of ways: "They [the other sheep] are not 'saints' or sanctified ones. . . . However, . . . they are sanctified for the warfare and must aid in keeping the camp of the theocratic warriors clean, unworldly, pleasing to God." It is clear, however, that this latter kind of sanctification is not the sanctification of which the Bible speaks.

by the grace of God shown to unworthy sinners, but rather by his own demonstration of his worthiness to be saved.

William J. Schnell points out that during his years with the movement the other sheep were told that if they stayed close to the Watchtower organization, listened attentively to its indoctrination, went out regularly to distribute literature, and rigidly reported the time spent in doing so, they *might* be saved at Armageddon! All the emphasis, he insists, was on works, particularly on witnessing, as the way to arrive at a reasonable certainty of future salvation, rather than on faith in Jesus Christ as Saviour.[321] Kurt Hutten similarly suggests that the real core of the way of salvation for Jehovah's Witnesses is witnessing; the harder one works at his witnessing, the more prominent the role he will play in the earthly paradise to come![322]

One more observation should be made. By their sharp division of believers into two classes, the Watchtower Society actually makes a large part of the Bible, particularly of the New Testament, meaningless for the majority of its adherents. For all Scriptural passages dealing with regeneration, sanctification, anointing, and consecration; all passages which speak of being sealed by the Spirit, filled with the Spirit, or testified to by the Spirit; all passages which describe the body of Christ, the bride of Christ, the new creation, the holy nation, and the elect (the list is far from exhaustive) are intended, so the Witnesses say, only for the anointed class and mean nothing for the other sheep. Surely this is a kind of divisive criticism of the Bible that is just as damaging to its authority and comfort as are the irreverent scissors of the higher critic!

DOCTRINE OF THE CHURCH AND SACRAMENTS

DOCTRINE OF THE CHURCH

The attitude of Jehovah's Witnesses toward the Christian church in general is so utterly bigoted as to be almost unbelievable. They — the Witnesses — alone are God's true people; all others are followers of the devil. The "great whore" of Revelation 17, as we saw, is organized religion, Christian as well as heathen.[323] The devil's organization, constantly at war against Jehovah's theo-

---

[321] *Op. cit.,* p. 104.
[322] *Seher, Gruebler, Enthusiasten,* p. 108.
[323] *Religion for Mankind,* p. 328.

cratic organization, has two parts: an invisible section, consisting of the demons, and a visible section. The latter section includes all the political organizations of this world and all its religious systems, including apostate Christendom — that is, all of Christendom except for the Watchtower Society and its members.[324] Though the Roman Catholic Church is singled out as the false church in its worst form,[325] all denominations of Christendom are included in the devil's organization.[326] Organized Christianity, especially from the fourth century onward, was the beginning of the "man of lawlessness"; the various Protestant denominations have now joined with the Roman Catholic Church in "making up that great combine, the organized clergy of Christendom, the 'man of lawlessness.' "[327] The religious clergy, in fact, are the direct visible link between mankind and the invisible demons![328]

True religion, according to *Religion for Mankind,* was established in the Garden of Eden before man fell (pp. 44-47); false religion, however, was introduced by Satan when he tempted Eve (pp. 49-53). In various ways false religion and apostasy revealed itself before the flood (pp. 58-74), after the flood (pp. 74-91), and during the later history of Israel (pp. 177-190). The Babylon from which the Jewish remnant was delivered in 537 B.C. foreshadowed the deliverance of the present-day true church, that is, the Jehovah-Witness organization, from modern Babylon, that is, the false religions of the present world, including particularly organized Christendom (p. 190; cf. p. 328). Jesus Christ again introduced true religion, but very soon apostasy began once more.[329] The Council of Nicaea in A.D. 325, which defined the doctrine of the Trinity, was a great victory for apostate Christianity.[330] Virtually the entire history of the Christian church through the ancient and medieval periods was a history of apostasy.[331] Though the Reformation brought some reforms, various gross errors, such as the Trinity, the immortality of the soul, and hell-fire,

---

[324] *Ibid.,* p. 307.
[325] *Ibid.,* pp. 272-77.
[326] *Jehovah's Witnesses in the Divine Purpose,* pp. 107-9.
[327] *Qualified to be Ministers,* pp. 288, 291.
[328] *The Kingdom is at Hand,* p. 186.
[329] *Qualified to be Ministers,* pp. 283-84.
[330] *The Truth Shall Make You Free,* p. 281; cf. *Religion for Mankind,* pp. 271-72.
[331] *Qualified to be Ministers,* pp. 283-291.

continued to be perpetuated.[332] The real restoration of the church to true religion did not take place until the 1870's when Russell began his Bible class;[333] the complete release of God's true people from "Babylonish captivity," however, did not occur until 1919.[334]

Basic to Jehovah-Witness ecclesiology is, once again, the distinction between the anointed class and the other sheep. We shall therefore look at each of these classes in turn.

The Anointed Class. This designates the "congregation of faithful Christians who [will] win the heavenly reward."[335] The number of this group, when completed, will be 144,000.[336] Since only the 144,000 properly belong to the church, or "congregation," as it is usually called,[337] it is clear that the true church of Jehovah will have only 144,000 members. Whenever the expression "congregation of God" occurs in Jehovah-Witness literature, therefore, it must be understood as referring only to the 144,000.

A rather bewildering variety of names are, however, applied to this group. Among these are the following: Anointed, Body of Christ, Bride of Christ, Chosen Ones, Elect, Holy Nation, Israel of God, Kingdom Class, Little Flock, New Creation, New Nation, Royal House, Royal Priesthood, Sanctuary Class, Sons of Levi, Spirit-Begotten, Spiritual Israel, Spiritual Sons.[338]

The relationship of this group to the heavenly theocratic organization has been previously described.[339] Because the heavenly theocratic organization is "God's woman" or "wife," and because the members of the anointed class are children of this woman, they can properly be said to be children of God. The anointed class

---

[332] *Ibid.*, p. 292.

[333] *Ibid.*, p. 296.

[334] *Ibid.*, p. 297. See references to this date in various Watchtower publications. The implication of all this is obvious: anyone who does not join the Jehovah-Witness organization today but remains in a Christian church is a devotee of false religion.

[335] *Your Will Be Done*, p. 15.

[336] See above, p. 51.

[337] "Scripturally 'church' means a congregation called out from the world for God's purpose; and so the *New World Translation* renders the Greek Word *ekklesia* by the English word 'congregation'" (*Let God Be True*, p. 125).

[338] *Watch Tower Publications Index of Subjects Discussed and Scriptures Explained, 1930-1960* (Pub. in 1961), p. 64. Note that the term "elect" is applied only to the 144,000. It will be remembered that the living members of this group existing on earth at any time are called the "remnant."

[339] See above, p. 54. It will be remembered that the anointed class began to be gathered at Pentecost.

is the earthly counterpart of Jehovah's heavenly theocratic organization, and hence plays a leading role in directing the activities of the Watchtower Society.

As will be described more fully under the DOCTRINE OF THE LAST THINGS, the anointed class is destined to spend eternity in heaven with Christ; they will not live in the Paradise of the new earth.

The Other Sheep. Charles T. Russell had already distinguished between two classes of spirit-begotten people: A higher class, which he called class *n,* the members of which will be the Bride of Christ, the "little flock," and will sit with the Lord in his throne in glory; and a lower class, which he called class *m,* who shrink from the death of the human will and therefore will not sit with the Lord in his throne of glory, but will finally reach birth as spirit beings of an order lower than the divine nature. This latter group Russell called, in fact, the "Great Company," a name very similar to one of the names given the "other sheep" class today: "the great crowd."[340] There are important differences, however, between these two classes as described by Russell and the two classes distinguished by Jehovah's Witnesses today. For Russell both of these classes were spirit-begotten; for Jehovah's Witnesses, however, the other sheep, or lower class, cannot be spirit-begotten. Russell taught that the members of the *m* class would eventually become spirit beings, whereas the Witnesses say that the other sheep will never become spirit beings. If Russell was once considered the mouthpiece of God, he is obviously no longer considered such by present-day Jehovah's Witnesses.[341]

Russell had also taught that at the end of the "time of harvest" in 1918 the door to immortality would be closed since every place in the bride class would be taken.[342] Because large numbers came into the movement after that date, however, Jehovah's Witnesses began to gather in addition to the anointed class another group,

---

[340] *Studies in the Scripture,* Series I, *The Plan of the Ages* (orig. pub. 1886; this ed. pub. in Allegheny, Pa., in 1907), pp. 235-36, 240.
[341] At this point a significant question arises: If Russell's teachings on a matter like the above can be so changed, what right do Jehovah's Witnesses have to follow him as slavishly as they do on other points? (see Martin and Klann, *op. cit.,* pp. 37-41). Suppose he were wrong on other matters as well!
[342] *Op cit.,* Series III, *Thy Kingdom Come* (orig. pub. 1891; this ed. pub. in Allegheny, Pa., in 1907), pp. 205-23; cf. Kurt Hutten, *Seher, Gruebler, Enthusiasten,* p. 104.

called "other sheep," in 1931.[343]   In 1936, it is said, the Watchtower Society received clear Scriptural evidence that this "other
sheep" class was destined to live on earth after Armageddon.[344]

As was the case with the anointed class, various names have
been given to this second class of believers.   The name "great
multitude" or "great crowd" is derived from Revelation 7:9,
where, so it is alleged, this group is distinguished from the 144,000
mentioned in the fourth verse of the chapter.[345]   The name "other
sheep" is derived from John 10:16, where Jesus is recorded as
saying, "other sheep I have, which are not of this fold."[346]   Another common name for this group is "Jonadabs," a name derived
from II Kings 10:15-28, and Jeremiah 35.   Jonadab (or Jehona-
dab), a son of Rechab, was the head of a Kenite tribe which
dwelt among the Israelites.   Jehu took Jonadab along with him
and used his help in suppressing Baal worship in Samaria.   Jonadab was thus a person who was not an Israelite, but who assisted
in the work of an Israelite king.[347]   Comparably, Jonadabs today
are not regarded as brethren in Christ, but nevertheless may be
spared from the destruction of Armageddon if they work along
with the anointed class.

Jehovah's Witnesses display a fantastic kind of exegetical ingenuity in finding Biblical symbols or types for the "other sheep"
class.   In *You May Survive Armageddon,* for example, the other
sheep are said to be pictured by the famine-stricken Egyptians
(pp. 328-29), the foreigners of David's army (pp. 251-52), the
Gibeonites (pp. 241-44), Jephthah's daughter (pp. 323-25),
Joseph's ten half-brothers (pp. 327-28), the mariners with Jonah
(pp. 149-150), the mixed company that left Egypt (pp. 122-25),
the Nethinim, non-Israelites who became temple slaves (pp. 142-
48), Noah's sons and daughters-in-law (pp. 290-93), the prodi-
gal son (p. 363), and Rebekah's nurse (pp. 224, 226, 229. Pp.
367-68 of this volume, in fact, list 42 Biblical types of the other
sheep!).

The other sheep whom Christ is gathering now are, however,
just the beginning of this group.   The vast majority of these other
sheep will be gathered during the millennium, when most of those

---

343 *Jehovah's Witnesses in the Divine Purpose,* p. 139; *New Heavens and
a New Earth,* p. 308; *Paradise Lost,* p. 195.
344 *Jehovah's Witnesses in the Divine Purpose,* p. 140.
345 *You May Survive Armageddon,* p. 180.
346 *Ibid.,* p. 68; *Let God Be True,* p. 231.
347 *You May Survive Armageddon,* pp. 276-81; *Let God Be True,* p. 231.

in the grave will be raised.[348]   During Christ's thousand-year reign the other sheep become "the earthly children of the Lifegiver Jesus Christ and hence are technically in the position of being 'grandchildren' of God."[349]

As will be set forth more fully under the DOCTRINE OF THE LAST THINGS, the other sheep will not get to heaven after death, but will be raised with physical bodies and will, if they pass the necessary tests, spend eternity in the Paradise of the new earth.

Reflecting upon Jehovah-Witness ecclesiology, we observe that, whereas the Scriptures say that there is one body and that we have been called to one hope of our calling (Ephesians 4:4), Jehovah's Witnesses have split the church[350] into two bodies, with two separate and distinct hopes for the future.   Whereas the Scriptures say, "You are all, in fact, sons of God through your faith in Christ Jesus" (Gal. 3:26, NWT), the Witnesses say, Among those who believe, some are sons of God, but others are grandsons of God.   Whereas the Scriptures say, of those who are in Christ, "There is neither Jew nor Greek, there is neither slave nor freeman, there is neither male nor female; for you are all one [person] in union with Christ Jesus (Galatians 3:28, NWT), the Watchtower says, There is, however, a most important distinction among the people of God which Paul here has forgotten to mention: that between the anointed class and the other sheep.   Whereas the Scriptures say, in Revelation 21:2, that the holy city comes down out of heaven from God, prepared as a bride adorned for her husband (implying that this bride will be on the new earth thereafter, so that heaven and earth now become one), Jehovah's Witnesses, in defiance of Scripture, wish to keep the bride of Christ in heaven throughout eternity, and to leave the lower class of adherents on earth.   Whereas the Scriptures say that Jesus Christ gave himself for us that he might "cleanse for himself a people peculiarly his own, zealous for fine works" (Titus 2:14, NWT), Watchtower teachers say that Christ really came to cleanse for himself not one people, but two peoples, and that these two peoples shall remain

---

[348] *You May Survive Armageddon,* p. 168.

[349] *Let God Be True,* p. 163.   This would imply that the other sheep are not children of God, but only grandchildren.   Inconsistently, however, Watchtower authors say elsewhere that the other sheep will remain forever on the new earth as "the justified human sons of Jehovah God" (*New Heaven and a New Earth,* p. 356).

[350] It is granted that, according to Watchtower teaching, only the 144,000 constitute the church.   But surely this kind of terminological jugglery does not justify their chopping the people of God into two severed fragments!

forever separate. I conclude that the ecclesiology of the Jehovah's Witnesses is a perversion of Scriptural teaching about the church.

DOCTRINE OF THE SACRAMENTS

Baptism. Baptism by immersion is required of all converts.[351] Any male Jehovah's Witness may perform this rite.[352] Conventions and assemblies of the Witnesses are usually occasions for mass baptisms. Candidates must be baptized "in the name of the Father and of the Son and of the holy spirit." This means that the person to be baptized must recognize Jehovah as Supreme, must recognize the part the Son performs in Jehovah's purpose, and must recognize the holy spirit as God's active force which will help him carry out his dedication.[353]

What is the significance of baptism? Baptism is defined in *Make Sure of All Things* as "an outward symbol, as a testimony before witnesses, of the baptized one's complete, unreserved and unconditional dedication and agreement to do the will of Jehovah God. . ." (p. 27). Immersion is essential to the symbolism: "The being dipped under water pictures the death of one's past course. The being lifted out of it pictures being raised and made alive to the doing of God's will."[354] Infant baptism is said to be unscriptural since repentance and faith must precede baptism.[355] Though the children of Jehovah's Witnesses are therefore not to be baptized in infancy, they must yet be treated by their parents as "something 'holy' to God."[356]

For all those who submit to this rite, baptism is a symbol of one's dedication to be God's minister.[357] This would therefore be true for both the anointed class and the other sheep. The other sheep, however, enjoy, in addition to their water baptism, a baptism into the Greater Noah.[358] This baptism means that they will be en-

[351] *Let God Be True*, p. 297; cf. *New Heavens and a New Earth*, p. 301; *Make Sure of All Things*, p. 30.
[352] *The Kingdom is At Hand*, p. 296.
[353] *Let God Be True*, pp. 297-98.
[354] *Ibid.*, p. 297.
[355] *Make Sure of All Things*, pp. 32, 30.
[356] *This Means Everlasting Life*, p. 256. The Scripture reference given here is I Cor. 7:14.
[357] *Make Sure of All Things*, p. 265. It will be remembered that every active Witness is called a minister, even though he does not devote full time to his witnessing.
[358] *New Heavens and a New Earth*, p. 309. Baptism into the Greater Noah is described on p. 293 of *You May Survive Armageddon* as baptism into Jesus Christ.

abled to survive Armageddon, provided they remain loyal to God.[359]

For the anointed class, moreover, there is also a baptism additional to their water baptism. This is "another baptism which no human being on earth can administer. This is the baptism of the holy spirit, which Christ Jesus administers as Jehovah's Servant."[360] This baptism of the holy spirit (sometimes called a baptism with the holy spirit) indicates that the person has been baptized into the body of Christ, and that he has been baptized into Christ's death.[361] This baptism into Christ's death means baptism into a kind of death that parts with all prospect of perfect human life in the new world.[362]

The other sheep, however, do not receive this baptism *of* or *with* the holy spirit, though "they do enjoy a measure of God's spirit."[363] They are not members of Christ's body, and are not baptized into Christ's death. They do not inherit God's kingdom,[364] or become part of it,[365] and they can only be the *subjects* of the kingdom of God,[366] over whom Christ and the 144,000 will rule eternally.

The Lord's Supper. Jehovah's Witnesses celebrate the Lord's Supper once a year, after sundown on the "exact day of the year that he [Christ] died, the true Passover date of the Jews. This would be Abib or Nisan 14."[367] This date usually occurs within what we call passion week; yet it may fall on any day of the week.[368]

Though at first the Bible Students called this meal the "Anniversary Supper," today Witnesses call it the "Memorial."[369] At this Memorial unleavened bread and fermented wine are served.[370] Jehovah's Witnesses reject transubstantiation (the view that the bread and wine change into the actual body and blood of Christ), maintaining that the loaf of bread merely symbolizes Jesus' fleshly body and that the cup of wine symbolizes Jesus' blood.[371]

[359] *New Heavens and a New Earth*, p. 311.
[360] *The Kingdom is at Hand*, p. 296.
[361] *Ibid.*, pp. 296-98.
[362] *New Heavens and a New Earth*, p. 309.
[363] *Ibid.*
[364] *Let God Be True*, p. 138.
[365] *Ibid.*, p. 136.
[366] *Ibid.*, pp. 138-39; *This Means Everlasting Life*, p. 275.
[367] *Jehovah's Witnesses in the Divine Purpose*, p. 24.
[368] *Make Sure of All Things*, p. 169.
[369] *Jehovah's Witnesses in the Divine Purpose*, p. 24.
[370] *Your Will Be Done*, p. 155; *Make Sure of All Things*, p. 260.
[371] *Make Sure of All Things*, p. 257.

When we look at the purpose of the Memorial, it becomes quite clear that it is intended for the 144,000 only. Its purpose, according to *Make Sure of All Things,* is to help the communicant remember Jesus' sacrifice (p. 260), whereby the forgiveness of sins has been obtained (pp. 261-62), and whereby a way has been opened for him and for his fellow anointed ones to go to heaven (p. 261). The communicant remembers that Jesus' blood put into force a new covenant between Jehovah and the 144,000 (p. 261), and thus exercises partnership with his fellow communicants and with Jehovah and Christ Jesus (p. 262).

It is specifically taught that Jesus "set up this evening meal with those who were to be taken into the covenant for the Kingdom."[372] A few lines farther along we read that the " 'other sheep' have personal Scriptural evidence that they are not in that Kingdom covenant."[373] In other words, the Memorial was intended by Christ to be celebrated by the 144,000 only! The only semblance of Scripture proof given for this limitation of the Memorial to the anointed class is the quotation of Luke 22:28-30 in the *New World Translation,* according to which Jesus makes a covenant with his disciples for a Kingdom. In utterly arbitrary fashion, the authors proceed to assert dogmatically that the other sheep have no part in this "Kingdom covenant." Thus Jehovah's Witnesses prohibit the vast majority of their adherents from partaking of a sacrament which Christ appointed for all His people.

Though the other sheep may not partake of the elements, they are instructed to attend the Memorial annually and to observe its celebration.[374] Thus the number of partakers of the Memorial is always a very small portion of those who attend. In 1971, for example, though there was a world-wide Memorial attendance of 3,453,542, only 10,384 partook of the meal.[375]

DOCTRINE OF THE LAST THINGS

INDIVIDUAL ESCHATOLOGY

The State of Man After Death. It has been shown above that Jehovah's Witnesses deny the immortality of the soul, define soul as a living person, and say that man does not possess a soul but

[372] *Your Will Be Done,* p. 156.
[373] *Ibid.* We are not told what this "personal Scriptural evidence" is.
[374] *Make Sure of All Things,* p. 263.
[375] *Watchtower,* Jan. 1, 1972, p. 25.

is a soul.[376] It will be obvious, therefore, that they disavow any conscious existence of the soul after death. Let us look into this matter a bit more in detail.

This disavowal is explicitly stated in a booklet published in 1955 entitled *What Do the Scriptures Say about "Survival After Death"?* On page 26 of this booklet they affirm that the human soul cannot exist apart from the human body. The human soul, therefore, is not immortal but mortal; a number of Scripture passages are cited in proof of this point (pp. 35-43). It is further contended that, since there is no sense in which any aspect of man continues to exist consciously after death, "in this respect mankind, because of the condemnation to death that they inherited from Adam, are like the lower animals that die. . ." (p. 31).[377]

The Meaning of Sheol and Hades. In this connection we should note what Jehovah's Witnesses teach about such Biblical words as Sheol and Hades. The Hebrew word Sheol, rendered *hell, grave,* or *pit* in the King James Version, means "mankind's common grave or the pit of burial"; it is emphatically denied that the word Sheol can ever mean "a fiery place of torture or a place of two compartments, one of bliss and one of fiery torment."[378] A number of Scripture passages are adduced to support this contention.[379] It is further asserted that Hades, the Greek equivalent of Sheol, also means "mankind's common grave."[380] Since the Bible teaches that after death man goes to either Sheol or Hades, and since both of these words simply mean grave, the Scriptures, so it is claimed, do not teach that there is any immaterial aspect of man which survives after death. When man dies, he totally ceases to exist.

Conditional Immortality. It must not be inferred from the

---

[376] See above, pp. 55-57.

[377] The similarity between this view of the state after death and that of the Seventh-day Adventists is quite apparent. Note that, as in the case of Seventh-day Adventist teaching, the Jehovah-Witness position on the state after death cannot properly be described as *soul-sleep,* since, according to them, there is no soul that sleeps after death. The soul simply ceases to exist after death; hence their view, like that of the Adventists, can more accurately be described as *soul-extinction.*

[378] *Let God Be True,* pp. 89-90.

[379] *Ibid.,* pp. 90-92. The Witnesses are not wholly consistent on this point, however. For on pp. 93-94 we are told that the hell pictured in Isa. 14:9, into which the king of Babylon — who stands for Satan — is said to descend, is the abyss into which Satan is cast at the beginning of the millennium (Rev. 20:1-3). The word here translated hell is, however, Sheol. In this instance Sheol obviously does not mean grave, since the devil has no body which can be cast into a grave.

[380] *Ibid.,* p. 93.

above description of the state of man after death, however, that, according to Watchtower teaching, death is the final end for every human being. The Witnesses do indeed maintain that this is so for certain men, as will be shown later. But they also affirm that for most members of the human race some type of existence after death is to be expected. This type of existence, however, is not a continued subsistence, either in conscious or unconscious fashion, of the soul, but will take the form of some kind of resurrection. This resurrection may occur in either a physical or a non-physical way. The members of the anointed class have been or will be "resurrected" as spirits with "bodies" that are spiritual but not in any sense physical. The members of the other sheep, however, as well as the vast majority of the rest of mankind, will be raised with physical bodies during the millennium.[381]

We thus observe that Jehovah's Witnesses, while denying the inherent immortality of the human soul, do teach a kind of conditional immortality. *Conditional immortality* may be defined as the view that holds that, though man is inherently mortal, immortality is conferred on certain members of the human race as a divine gift. The Witnesses teach that immortality belongs primarily and originally to Jehovah.[382] Immortality in a secondary sense (not *inherent* but *bestowed* immortality), however, is given only to Christ and to the members of the anointed class:

> Christ Jesus was first to receive immortality as a reward for his faithful course on earth, and it [immortality] is now also given in reward to those who are of the true congregation or "body of Christ." Immortality is a reward for faithfulness.[383]

This does not mean, however, that all other human beings besides the anointed class will finally be annihilated. The other sheep and the majority of the rest of mankind will be raised with physical bodies; after they shall have passed the tests to which they must submit during the millennium, they will be granted everlasting life. But this everlasting life should be distinguished from immortality, which is bestowed only on the anointed class.[384] For Jehovah's Witnesses, to receive immortality, therefore, means to

---

[381] These teachings will be examined in greater detail and carefully documented later in this chapter.

[382] *Make Sure of All Things*, p. 349.

[383] *Let God Be True*, p. 74. Cf. *Make Sure of All Things*, pp. 136, 350, 246, 247.

[384] *Make Sure of All Things*, pp. 248, 243. Cf. *Let God Be True*, p. 75.

be "raised" without a physical body; everlasting life in a physical body is not considered equivalent to immortality.[385]

In summary, we may say that, according to Watchtower teaching, one of four possible destinies awaits a person when he dies: (1) he may remain in the condition of nonexistence into which death has plunged him: (2) he may be "raised" with a "spirit body," thus receiving immortality, after which he will go directly to heaven to reign there with Christ; (3) he may be raised with a physical body and then, after having passed the millennial tests, receive everlasting life on the renewed earth; or (4) he may, after having been raised with a physical body, still fail to pass the millennial tests, and thus eventually be annihilated.[386]

GENERAL ESCHATOLOGY

The Kingdom of God. In order to understand Jehovah-Witness teaching about the so-called "second presence" of Christ, we must first examine their doctrine of the kingdom of God. Here, too, we shall find the Witnesses differing sharply from evangelical Christians. Let us look first at a rather comprehensive definition of the kingdom of God:

> The Kingdom of God is a Sovereign-empowered theocratic government under an administration of divinely appointed Kings. Jehovah himself is the great Everlasting King. . . . He has taken into association as co-regent his Son Christ Jesus. God has purposed the Kingdom as the capital or ruling part of his universal organization. It is comprised of the King Christ Jesus and 144,000 associate kings taken from among men. It is entirely heavenly, having no earthly part. All becoming members must be resurrected and given spirit bodies.[387]

From this definition we learn that, though Jehovah is the King of this kingdom, Jesus Christ is His co-regent and that this kingdom is the "ruling part" of Jehovah's organization. It is also quite clear from this statement that only the 144,000 belong to this

---

[385] Cf. what was said on p. 57 above about the everlasting life Adam would have attained if he had not sinned. Quite inconsistent with this position, however, is the denial of the immortality of the angels, who, like the glorified members of the anointed class, do not have physical bodies (see above, pp. 57-58).

[386] See Appendix E in *The Four Major Cults* for a critical evaluation of Jehovah-Witness teaching on soul-extinction, conditional immortality, and the annihilation of the wicked.

[387] *Make Sure of All Things*, p. 226.

kingdom. Even the 144,000, however, do not belong to the kingdom until after their "resurrection" with spirit bodies. The kingdom of God, therefore, is in no sense earthly; it is exclusively a heavenly kingdom.[388]

When we now ask Jehovah's Witnesses when this heavenly kingdom was established, we get the following kind of answer: God foretold the coming of this kingdom in Old Testament times, the first of these prophecies being Genesis 3:15.[389] During the history of Israel, God set up a theocracy, in which He Himself was the ruler of His people; this, however, was not the kingdom promised in Eden, but only a picture or type of the greater kingdom that was to come.[390] When Christ came he proclaimed that the kingdom of God had drawn near; this, however, did not mean that the kingdom had actually been established, but only that the anointed king was now personally in the midst of the people of Israel.[391] Though the disciples also proclaimed the presence of the kingdom in this sense at the time when Christ was upon earth, "there is no record that they continued to do so after his [Jesus'] ascension on high," since "such an announcement would not be appropriate until his return and second presence."[392] Christ, therefore, did not establish the kingdom of God at the time of his first advent. Neither did he establish this kingdom at once after he had ascend-

[388] The kingdom of God, therefore, for the Witnesses, does not designate a group of people on earth — this despite the fact that they name their places of worship "Kingdom Halls." It is specifically stated that "all selected for the kingdom must die in order to enter it" (*ibid.*, p. 235). Though the kingdom of God is a heavenly organization, this kingdom does have earthly subjects: the other sheep (*Let God Be True*, p. 139; *This Means Everlasting Life*, p. 275). Since only the 144,000 are members of the kingdom, the other sheep are subjects but not members. Even the angelic hosts who serve as faithful messengers of the king are not members of this kingdom but only subjects (*Let God Be True*, p. 138).
[389] *Let God Be True*, p. 134.
[390] *Ibid.*, p. 135.
[391] *Ibid.*, p. 140. In this connection Lk. 17:21 is quoted: "Look, the kingdom of God is in your midst" (NWT). The Witnesses evade the clear teaching of this passage — that the kingdom of God had then already been established — by contending that these words only mean that the King of the kingdom was then in the midst of the Pharisees (cf. also *The Truth Shall Make You Free*, p. 299).
[392] *Let God Be True*, p. 140. But how would Jehovah's Witnesses interpret Acts 8:12, where Philip's preaching to the Samaritans is described as "preaching good tidings concerning the kingdom of God"; or Acts 19:8, where Paul is said to have taught in the synagogue at Ephesus for three months, "reasoning and persuading as to the things concerning the kingdom of God"?

ed into heaven; his ascension was only the beginning of a long period of waiting for the establishment of the kingdom of God.[393]

When, then, was the kingdom of God actually established? In the year A.D. 1914. We have previously noted the fantastic calculations whereby the Witnesses have arrived at this date.[394] On October 1 of the year 1914, it is contended, the "appointed times of the nations" ended, and God's heavenly kingdom, with Christ enthroned as king, began.[395] It can therefore now properly be said that the kingdom of God is here.[396] Since the kingdom of God is here, we are now living in the "time of the end" — a period which began in 1914 and will end when the devil's world is destroyed in the Battle of Armageddon.[397]

The "Return" of Jesus Christ. Since Jehovah's Witnesses identify the establishment of the kingdom of God with the "return" of Jesus Christ, we next turn our attention to this "return." I have put quotation marks around the word *return* for two reasons: (1) This so-called "return" of Christ was neither a physical nor a visible one, since Christ after his resurrection has no physical body[398]; and (2) this was not really a "return" at all, since Christ did not go back to earth but simply began to rule over his kingdom from heaven.[399] Thus there is actually no resemblance whatever between Jehovah-Witness teaching on the "return" of Christ and evangelical Protestant teaching about Christ's Second Coming.[400]

To understand better what the Witnesses mean by Christ's "return," let us compare two statements from their writings. The

---

[393] *The Truth Shall make you Free,* p. 241; *Let God Be True,* p. 140; *Make Sure of All Things,* p. 234. See also *New Heavens and a New Earth,* pp. 315, 317; and *This Means Everlasting Life,* p. 220.

[394] See above, pp. 41-43.

[395] *Paradise Lost,* pp. 173-74. Cf. *You May Survive Armageddon,* p. 100; *Let God Be True,* p. 141.

[396] *Let God Be True,* p. 141.

[397] *Paradise Lost,* pp. 178, 203. Further details about the nature and functioning of this kingdom will be given as we go along.

[398] *Let God Be True,* pp. 198-99; *Make Sure of All Things,* p. 321.

[399] *Paradise Lost,* pp. 173-74; *New Heavens and a New Earth,* p. 317.

[400] Watchtower publications usually prefer the designation "second presence" (using the word *presence* as a translation of the Greek word *parousia*), but they occasionally speak of Christ's *return* (*Let God Be True,* p. 198; *Make Sure of All Things,* p. 319). If, however, Christ was already in heaven prior to 1914, and if in 1914 he simply assumed a throne in heaven, how can this action possibly be called a *return?* The word *return* is used meaningfully when a return to earth is thought of, but it has no intelligible meaning when it is used to describe the Jehovah-Witness conception of the "second presence" of Christ.

first, from *This Means Everlasting Life,* p. 220, reads: "When he [Christ] ascended to heaven he sat down at God's right hand to wait for that time of entering into his authority and ruling like Melchizedek over his enemies as his footstool." The second is from *You May Survive Armageddon,* p. 100: ". . . Jehovah the heavenly Father brought forth his kingdom by bringing forth his anointed King-Priest Jesus Christ and elevating him to the active kingship in the throne at God's right hand." Putting these two statements together, we learn that from the time of his ascension to October 1, 1914 (when the kingdom was brought forth), Christ was sitting at the right hand of God the Father, and that on October 1, 1914, the Father placed the Son on the throne at His right hand. Thus the "return" or "second presence" of Christ simply means that Christ, who had been sitting at the Father's right hand in heaven since his ascension, now ascends the throne of his kingdom at the Father's right hand in heaven. The "return" of Christ is, for Jehovah's Witnesses, an exclusively heavenly transaction, consisting merely in Christ's exchanging an "ordinary" [401] seat at the Father's right hand for a throne. Watchtower teachings on this point, therefore, not only deny Christ's physical and visible return to earth, but also imply that Christ did not exercise His kingly office prior to 1914.

According to Jehovah-Witness teaching, therefore, we need no longer look for Christ's "return" or "second presence," because this "return" has already taken place. Christ "became King of the earth at the time of his second presence, A.D. 1914."[402]

This "second presence" of Christ, however, was also the occasion for an upheaval in the demonic world. Jehovah's Witnesses see in Revelation 12:1-9 a description of events which occurred at the time of this "second presence." The birth of the man-child depicted in verse 5 symbolically pictures the birth of the heavenly kingdom and the placing of Christ on the throne of this kingdom.[403]

[401] By what stretch of the imagination, however, can Jehovah's Witnesses interpret the Biblical phrase "sitting at the right hand of God" as designating anything less than Christ's kingly reign from heaven? See I Pet. 3:22 and Eph. 1:20-23.
[402] *Make Sure of All Things,* p. 234. It should be noted that on this point present-day Jehovah's Witnesses are not true to the teachings of Russell who, as we have seen, taught that Christ's second presence began in the fall of 1874 (see above, p. 11). If Russell could be wrong about this crucial matter, how can the Witnesses be so sure that their present leaders are right about the new date?
[403] *New Heavens and a New Earth,* pp. 209-10.

The dragon's attempt to devour the man-child pictures the devil's unsuccessful endeavor to destroy the newborn government.[404] Since, for the Witnesses, Michael is another name for Christ in his glorified state, the war which is next described, between Michael and his angels on the one hand and the dragon and his angels on the other, is simply a dramatic picture of a great battle between Christ and the devil.[405] As a result of this great battle, the devil was hurled out of heaven and was cast down to the earth (v. 9).[406]

After Satan had been hurled out of heaven, however, he proceeded to vent his rage upon the peoples of the earth.

> Furious at the successful birth of the theocratic government, Satan determined to destroy all people ere they learned of the newly established kingdom. This was why he plunged the nations into the war of 1914-1918. It was the first time in history that so great a conflict had taken place.[407]

Driving home their point, the authors of *Let God Be True* go on to say: "It [the beginning of World War I] is conclusive proof that the 'appointed times' have ended, Satan's rule is interfered with, and the enthronement of Christ Jesus has taken place."[408]

Christ's Coming to His Temple. Though at the time when Christ became king of the heavenly kingdom of God in 1914 he ruled alone, it was not his intention to continue ruling as a solitary monarch. ". . . Men and women from upon the earth have been raised out of death to heavenly life to rule with him."[409] The number of the members of this group, we are further told, is to be 144,000; thus we know that those who either have or will have the privilege of ruling with Christ in this sense are the members of the anointed class. This group, however, did not begin to reign with Christ in heaven at the moment when the kingship was bestowed upon him, but a few years later.[410]

In explaining when the members of the anointed class did begin

---

[404] *Let God Be True*, p. 202.
[405] *Paradise Lost*, p. 176.
[406] *Ibid.*
[407] *Let God Be True*, p. 254.
[408] *Ibid.* It takes a bit of imagination to understand how the beginning of the worst war in history, fought largely by non-Jews, can be construed as proof that the "appointed times of the nations" — times during which Gentile nations would dominate the earth (see above, p. 41) — have ended, that Satan's rule has been interfered with, and that Christ's enthronement has now taken place!
[409] *Paradise Lost*, p. 213.
[410] *Ibid.*

to reign with Christ, the authors of *Paradise Lost* point to a parallel between Christ's first presence on earth and his "second presence." Christ was anointed with God's spirit — it is said — during his first presence in A.D. 29; three and a half years after this he cleansed the temple at Jerusalem; six days after this he arose from the dead. A similar time period, we are further told, is found during Jesus' "second presence." In the fall of 1914 he was crowned as king; three and a half years after that he cleansed Jehovah's spiritual temple; a very short time after the temple's cleansing, still in the year 1918, the heavenly resurrection of certain Christians occurred, and these then began to live and reign with Christ in heaven.[411]

Examining this matter in somewhat greater detail, we ask what Jehovah's Witnesses mean by the spiritual temple which Christ is supposed to have cleansed in 1918. This spiritual temple is understood to have been the Jehovah-Witness earthly organization, for we are told that during this year "Christians who had selfish hearts and wrong ideas toward his [Christ's] service dropped out of his organization."[412]

A short time after this cleansing of the spiritual temple, the members of the anointed class who had died by that time were "raised" with spiritual (that is, non-physical) bodies, and were placed on the throne with Jesus Christ.[413] At another place it is said that these risen ones were now "put in their places in the heavenly temple"[414]; from these words it appears that there is a temple in heaven corresponding to the earthly spiritual temple which Christ had just cleansed, and that the "raised" members of the anointed class are now in this heavenly temple — or, perhaps, constitute this temple.[415]

[411] *Ibid.*
[412] *Ibid.* See *Qualified to be Ministers*, pp. 313-14, where it is made clear that Jesus' coming to his temple for judgment in the spring of 1918 resulted in the separation of the "faithful and discreet slave" class from the "evil slave" group. The latter group, it is added, then subdivided and left the movement (see also *Jehovah's Witnesses in the Divine Purpose*, pp. 70-73). The above, in other words, is the official Jehovah-Witness explanation for the formation of certain schismatic groups in the year 1918 (see above, p. 15).
[413] *Paradise Lost*, p. 213; *New Heavens and a New Earth*, p. 319.
[414] *You May Survive Armageddon*, p. 117.
[415] There is a great deal of ambiguity in Jehovah-Witness writing about this heavenly temple. Often one gets the impression that this heavenly temple is simply another name for the 144,000 after they have been translated to heaven, and that this temple will only be completed after the last of the 144,000 have been "raised" from the dead: "Jehovah's

The Witnesses thus try to show that prophecy was fulfilled in 1918 as well as in 1914. Which prophecy? The prophecy of Malachi 3:1, "And suddenly there will come to his temple the [true] Lord, whom you people are seeking, and the messenger of the covenant in whom you are delighting" (NWT). There was, so they say, an "initial" or "miniature" fulfillment of this prophecy, and a final fulfillment. The initial fulfillment occurred when Christ cleansed the temple during his earthly ministry, and when certain subsequent events occurred.[416] The final fulfillment came in 1918, when Christ again came to his temple.[417]

In trying to show how this final fulfillment occurred, however, the Watchtower authors become quite badly confused. According to *Paradise Lost,* Christ's coming to the temple in 1918 was his coming to the earthly Jehovah-Witness organization to cleanse it of rebellious members.[418] According to the authors of *The Truth Shall Make You Free* and *You May Survive Armageddon,* however, the temple Christ came to in 1918 was not the earthly organization but the heavenly temple.[419] So there is ambiguity as to which temple he came to. Even if one understands Jehovah's Witnesses to mean by the temple to which Christ came in 1918 the heavenly one rather than the earthly organization, one is still at a loss to know exactly what they are trying to say. For, (1) if the heavenly temple is just another name for the 144,000, it is not correct to say that Christ came to them in 1918, for they were then "raised" to be with him in heaven; it would be more correct to say

---

temple . . . consists of more than Jesus alone. It includes his congregation of 144,000 spiritual members, the spiritual body of which Jesus Christ is Head" (*You May Survive Armageddon,* p. 81). Members of the anointed class are often described as "living stones" of that temple (*ibid.,* pp. 96, 108; *Let Your Name Be Sanctified,* p. 274). At other times, however, one receives the impression that this heavenly temple is a place in heaven to which the members of the anointed class go after they die: "They [the deceased anointed ones] are now with him [Christ] at the temple, that is, in the condition of unity with him in the place invisible to human eyes, which place is symbolized by the 'air'" (*The Truth Shall Make You Free,* p. 304).

[416] *You May Survive Armageddon,* pp. 91-97.
[417] *Ibid.,* pp. 98ff.; *The Truth Shall Make You Free,* pp. 303, 324.
[418] *Paradise Lost,* p. 213.
[419] *The Truth Shall Make You Free,* pp. 303-4; on p. 324. this coming to the heavenly temple is called Christ's *epiphaneia* or "appearing" in distinction from his *parousia,* which occurred in 1914. Cf. *You May Survive Armageddon,* pp. 103-4; on the latter page it is said that the resurrection of the sleeping temple stones took place shortly after the arrival of Adonai [the Lord] and His messenger at the spiritual temple on the heavenly Mount Zion.

that, in 1918, the temple came to Christ. If, however, (2) the heavenly temple is the name of a certain place in heaven, we wonder where this place is. From *New Heavens and a New Earth,* p. 319, we learn that the 144,000 who are "raised" "are by such a spiritual, heavenly resurrection granted to sit with Jesus Christ in his throne, even as he conquered this old world and sat down with his Father in His throne." These words imply that the place to which the "raised" 144,000 go is the place where Christ is (for Christ has been seated on the throne since 1914). If this is so, how can Christ be said to "come to his temple" in 1918? How can one "come to" a place where he already is?[420]

The "first resurrection." We should now examine in greater detail what Jehovah's Witnesses mean by the "resurrection" of the deceased members of the anointed class which occurred in 1918. The Witnesses distinguish between a *first* or *earlier* resurrection and later resurrections.[421] These resurrections, however, are distinguished not just in time but also in manner; the "first" or "earlier" resurrection is said to be a nonphysical one, whereas the later resurrections are said to be physical.

What is the nature of this "first resurrection"? The following rather lengthy quotation describes both types of resurrection:

> Resurrection is a restoration to life of the nonexistent dead. . . . It is an act of God dependent entirely upon God's marvelous power through Christ and upon His memory of the dead. It is the reactivating of the life pattern of the creature, a transcription of which is on record with God, and is referred to as being in His memory. Resurrection does not involve the restoring of the original identical body of the creature. The life pattern is the personal life-long record of the creature built up by his thoughts and by the experiences in the life he has lived resulting from certain habits, leanings, mental abilities, memories and

---

[420] On p. 275 of *This Means Everlasting Life* it is unequivocally asserted that the throne from which Christ rules in heaven is at the same time the place where he ministers in the heavenly temple: "It is from heaven that Christ and his 144,000 associate kings rule, for Christ Jesus sits at God's right hand. . . . The throne, heaven, is the place for kings to rule from, and not the footstool, the earth. Moreover, it is the Most Holy of all, the heaven itself of God's presence, where the High Priest of God applies the merit of his sacrifice for the sake of humankind."

[421] They call the "resurrection" of the 144,000 the "first resurrection," basing this on Rev. 20:6 (*Let God Be True,* p. 277); at times, however, they also refer to this as the "earlier resurrection," basing this designation on the NWT of Phil. 3:11, where the Greek word *exanastasis* is rendered, wholly without lexical warrant, *earlier resurrection* (*ibid.,* p. 282).

history. It is also a register of the individual's intellectual growth and his characteristics, all of which make up one's personality. Hence, according to God's will for the creature, in a resurrection one is restored or re-created in either a human or a spirit body and yet retains his personal identity by the setting in motion again of the distinctive life pattern of that individual.[422]

Note that resurrection is here defined as a restoration to life of the nonexistent dead, that it is dependent upon God's memory of the dead, that it is a reactivation of the life pattern of the creature rather than a restoring of the creature's original body, and that it is by this reactivation of the life pattern that the personal identity of the individual is to be retained. Note, too, that one may be restored in "either a human or a spirit body." In the "first resurrection" individuals are restored in *spirit bodies*.[423]

This "first resurrection" follows the pattern of Christ's resurrection. As he was "raised" without a physical body in order to partake of heavenly life, so also are the members of the anointed class. Only Christ and the 144,000, therefore, participate in this "first resurrection." When the Bible says that Christ is the "firstfruits of them which are asleep" (I Cor. 15:20), this does not mean that he was the firstfruits of all believers who have died, but only of the 144,000.[424]

This "first resurrection" was therefore not a bodily resurrection in the sense that these individuals were raised with physical bodies. It is called, as a matter of fact, a "spiritual, heavenly resurrection."[425] The members of the anointed class "raised" in 1918 are said to have been raised with "spirit bodies" to join Christ at the spiritual temple,[426] to have become "invisible spirit creatures,"[427] and to have entered upon "spirit life in the heavens."[428] We are, in fact, given the distinct impression that this "spirit

---

[422] *Make Sure of All Things,* p. 311.

[423] The expression "spirit body" will be puzzling to most readers. It will be recalled that, according to Watchtower teaching, a heavenly soul "consists of a body together with the life principle or life force actuating it" (above, p. 56). So there are "heavenly" bodies as well as earthly, physical bodies. The author was told by Mr. Ulysses Glass, a member of the Watchtower staff, that these "heavenly bodies" will be vastly superior to the bodies of those on earth (personal interview, June 6, 1962).

[424] *Let God Be True,* pp. 276-77.

[425] *New Heavens and a New Earth,* p. 319.

[426] *Let God Be True,* p. 203.

[427] *Ibid.,* p. 138.

[428] *Paradise Lost,* p. 231.

life" is a more perfect form of life than one which would involve a physical resurrection: "The 'resurrection of life' includes the 'first resurrection,' which is the resurrection to instantaneous perfection of life, spirit life, in which Jesus himself participated and in which only the 144,000 joint heirs participate with him."[429] Since this was a "resurrection" to a heavenly, spirit existence, it was invisible to human eyes.[430] In the case of those "raised" in 1918, this event was a transition from nonexistence to spirit-existence, possible only because God had on record a transcription of the life patterns of these individuals.[431] Actually, therefore, God re-created them on the basis of His memory of what they were like before they died.

Jehovah's Witnesses do not teach, however, that in 1918 the total number of the anointed class was "raised" with a spiritual resurrection. A "remnant" of the 144,000 was still alive in 1918; a "remnant" is still alive today; and there will be a "remnant" of this group left on earth during the coming millennium.[432] So the question arises: What happens to the members of this remnant when they die? The answer is: they undergo the "first resurrection" at the moment of their death. Immediately at death they enter into an "eternal spirit existence,"[433] are "resurrected in the spirit,"[434] are "changed instantaneously to spirits immortal, incorruptible,"[435] and "receive an immediate change to spirit life."[436] They are changed from being human creatures to being spirit creatures in heaven with Christ.[437] At another place we

---

[429] *You May Survive Armageddon*, pp. 354-55. One is tempted to ask: if perfection of life is spirit life, how could Jesus have lived a perfect life on earth in a body? One senses at this point a kind of Gnostic devaluation of the body.
[430] *Let God Be True*, p. 278; *The Kingdom is at Hand*, p. 304.
[431] Make Sure of All Things, pp. 311, 313.
[432] *Let God Be True*, p. 278; *Paradise Lost*, p. 231; *New Heavens and a New Earth*, p. 321. In the last-named reference it is specifically stated that "the thousand-year reign does not have to wait until they [the last of the remnant] are glorified in the heavens. . . ."
[433] *Let God Be True*, p. 129. In this connection the authors quote 1 Cor. 15:51-52, "We all shall not sleep but we shall all be changed, in a moment, in the twinkling of an eye, at the last trump. . ." (cf. *Paradise Lost*, p. 232). Apparently the "last trump" is thought to sound every time a member of the remnant dies!
[434] *Let God Be True*, p. 279.
[435] *This Means Everlasting Life*, p. 235.
[436] *Let God Be True*, p. 203. Cf. *This Means Everlasting Life*, p. 231; *Paradise Lost*, p. 231.
[437] *Paradise Lost*, p. 232.

are told: ". . . At death they are changed from human to divine, incorruptible, immortal, spiritual, in but a moment or twinkling of an eye. . . ."[438]

As this last quotation indicates ("changed from human to divine"), this "first resurrection" is a kind of deification of the members of the anointed class. This does not mean, of course, that the "little flock" now become equal to Jehovah God, but they do become virtually equal to Christ — who is also "divine," though not equal to Jehovah. Note the following parallels between what happens to the members of the anointed class and what happened to Christ: (1) Like Christ, they are "raised" with spirit bodies for life in heaven; (2) like Christ, they have sacrificed their rights to life on earth in order to earn the right to life in heaven;[439] (3) like Christ, they attain immortality — an immortality which is shared by no other creatures, not even the angels; (4) like Christ, they have been begotten by God's spirit to become spiritual sons of God; (5) like Christ, they reign after death from a heavenly throne. Thus, as has been previously observed,[440] the difference between Christ and the 144,000, for the Witnesses, is not one of kind but only one of degree. And at this point we may well wonder whether one is justified in affirming even a difference of degree![441]

In referring to this "first resurrection" I have been putting the word *resurrection* between quotation marks since I do not believe that this can properly be called a resurrection. I make this judgment for two reasons:

(1) As was noted in the case of the Seventh-day Adventists,[442] this is not really a resurrection because, at least in the case of those "raised" in 1918, these individuals had been completely annihilated when they died; hence it would be more accurate to call their "restoration" to life in 1918 a new creation.

(2) The word *resurrection* has always been understood by the Christian church to mean resurrection with a physical body.

---

[438] *New Heavens and a New Earth*, p. 320. Cf. *Make Sure of All Things*, p. 247, where we are told that Christ and the 144,000 in heaven share a "divine nature."

[439] See above, pp. 72, 75.

[440] See above, p. 65.

[441] On p. 275 of *This Means Everlasting Life* the astounding suggestion is made that the 144,000 must help to bring back the dead who are in the graves!

[442] See *The Four Major Cults*, p. 140.

Giving to people who had previously been annihilated a new existence as "spirit creatures" (or transforming people instantaneously from physical beings to "spirit creatures," in the case of those "raised" after 1918) is not a resurrection but rather a change into a different kind of existence.

In the history of the Christian church, people who taught that the "resurrection" was a nonphysical one were branded as heretics. The early fathers vigorously defended the resurrection of the body (in a physical sense) as a distinctively Christian doctrine over against those who, under the influence of Greek philosophy or Gnostic speculation, denied this teaching.[443] Yet today Jehovah's Witnesses, claiming to be listening to Scripture alone, are again reviving this ancient heresy!

It should now be added, by way of evaluation, that, as was observed in the case of the "resurrection" of Jesus Christ,[444] so here also there is no real continuity between the state of being in the flesh and the "resurrection" state. Christ by his "resurrection" was changed from a human being to a spirit creature. So it is with the 144,000: by their "resurrection" they are changed from being human creatures to being spirit creatures.[445] From their own description of this change, therefore, we learn that, for the Witnesses, the 144,000 cease to be human beings after their "resurrection." They enter into an entirely different kind of existence: a spirit existence. It would not be inaccurate to say that the 144,000 are, at death, changed into angels (angels, that is, who are now immortal, in distinction from ordinary angels, who remain mortal). The "resurrection" of the 144,000 is, therefore, really the creation of a new type of being — not a resurrection of human beings.

The Judgment of the Nations. Jehovah's Witnesses distinguish various *judgment days*.[446] One of these days of judgment began when Christ came to the temple in 1918.[447] "In the spring of

---

[443] See, e.g., Polycarp, *To The Philippians*, 7; *The Epistle of Barnabas*, 5 and 21; *II Clement*, 9; Justin Martyr, *First Apology*, 18-19; Tatian, *To the Greeks*, 6; Theophilus, *To Autolycus*, I, 7; Athenagoras, *The Resurrection of the Dead*, 18-25; Irenaeus, *Against Heresies*: II, 29, 2; IV, 5, 2.

[444] See above, p. 66.

[445] *Paradise Lost*, p. 232.

[446] *Make Sure of All Things*, pp. 219-25.

[447] *Let God Be True*, p. 277. We note here some similarity to the "investigative judgment" of the Seventh-day Adventists. It will be recalled that Russell had some early associations with the Adventists. As the

1918," it is said, "he [Christ] came as Jehovah's Messenger to the temple and began judgment first of the 'house of God' and then of the nations of this world."[448]

This judgment which began at the house of God is, however, variously interpreted. In one place we are told that this judgment was accomplished by the "resurrection" of the anointed class, by which a favorable judgment was rendered to the house of God.[449] At another place in the same book, however, we are informed that this judgment consisted in the following: The faithful ones who took up the witnessing work in 1918 and 1919, and who began to serve spiritual food to the spiritually hungry at this time, were judged by Jehovah to be the "faithful and discreet slave class." Thus, it is alleged, Jehovah indicated who were His true people, distinguishing them from those who falsely claimed to be the "house of God," namely, the churches of Christendom.[450] One may apparently adopt either interpretation, or both.

In the spring of 1918 Christ also began his judgment of the nations. This teaching is derived from Matthew 25:31-46, the passage which speaks of the judgment of the sheep and the goats.[451] This judgment, it is said, takes place during the "time of the end," that is, from the spring of 1918 to the Battle of Armageddon.[452] Christ, now seated on the throne of his glory, is busy separating the people of the nations into two classes, called sheep and goats.[453] The basis for this judgment is the attitude people take toward the kingdom message and its bearers, the remnant.[454] The goats are those who have no appreciation for the kingdom message and who show no help or kindness to the bearers of this message;[455] this group will include Christendom because it has had no charity for the remnant of Christ's broth-

---

Watchtower understanding of this judgment at the temple is unfolded, however, it will become evident that the teaching of the Witnesses here is quite different from that of Seventh-day Adventism.

[448] *Ibid.*, p. 287. In connection with the judgment which began at the "house of God," I Peter 4:17 is quoted.

[449] *You May Survive Armageddon*, p. 117.

[450] *Ibid.*, pp. 207-208. To understand what Jehovah's Witnesses mean by the "faithful and discreet slave class," see above, pp. 33-34.

[451] *Let God Be True*, p. 290.

[452] *You May Survive Armageddon*, p. 160.

[453] *Let God Be True*, p. 204.

[454] *Ibid.*, p. 290; *You May Survive Armageddon*, p. 163.

[455] *Let God Be True*, p. 290.

ers.[456] The sheep, however, are those who rejoice at the coming of the kingdom and do good to the remnant who bear the message.[457] By the time of the Battle of Armageddon this judging of the nations will have been completed; the sheep will have been gathered at the king's right side, into company with the remnant, whereas the goats will have been gathered at his left side.[458] At the Battle of Armageddon the judgment against the nations will be executed.[459] Then the goats will be destroyed and annihilated, whereas the sheep will live through the battle and "enter upon the opportunities for everlasting life in the new world."[460]

The Battle of Armageddon. Before the glorious new world can be ushered in, however, there will occur a battle more terrible than anything the world has ever seen. "Armageddon will be the worst thing ever to hit the earth within the history of man."[461] What kind of battle will this be?

We find a brief definition of it on page 24 of *Make Sure of All Things*:

> The battle of Jehovah God Almighty in which his executive officer Christ Jesus leads invisible forces of righteousness to destroy Satan and his demonic and human organization, eliminating wickedness from the universe and vindicating Jehovah's universal sovereignty.

From this definition we learn that Armageddon will be Jehovah's decisive (though not final) battle against His enemies, both demonic and human; that Christ will be Jehovah's executive officer, leading invisible forces to victory; and that this battle will result in the elimination of wickedness and the vindication of Jehovah's sovereignty.[462]

The background for the Battle of Armageddon is the tribulation brought upon Satan's world by Christ, who has taken action to

---

[456] *You May Survive Armageddon,* pp. 165-66.
[457] *Let God Be True,* p. 290; *You May Survive Armageddon,* pp. 164-65.
[458] *You May Survive Armageddon,* pp. 164-68.
[459] *Let God Be True,* p. 287.
[460] *You May Survive Armageddon,* pp. 165-67. The moral is obvious: if you want to survive Armageddon and enter the paradise of the new world, you must leave Christendom and join the Jehovah-Witness movement!
[461] Statement made by Nathan Knorr at the 1953 Yankee-Stadium Assembly, quoted in *You May Survive Armageddon,* p. 11.
[462] It will be recalled that the vindication of Jehovah's sovereignty is, for the Witnesses, the primary purpose of world history (see above, pp. 49-50).

unseat Satan from his position as ruler of the earth. Actual combat against Satan and his demon horde began with Christ's enthronement in A.D. 1914.   This combat was cut short in A.D. 1918, to be resumed at Armageddon.[463] "In between, while this tribulation is cut short, there is a work of proclaiming the Kingdom and its day of vengeance, and of exposing Satan's filthy organization. . . ."[464] Because it is believed that only those who are members of the Watchtower organization, whether as anointed ones or other sheep, will survive Armageddon,[465] and because it is further believed that no one who dies at Armageddon will be raised from the dead during the millennium,[466] Jehovah's Witnesses preach with great urgency: Come into Jehovah's theocratic organization now, or be forever annihilated in the Battle of Armageddon![467]

This great battle will not be a conflict between capitalism and communism, nor will it be a destruction of the nations through atomic energy, but it will be Jehovah's fight in which both the invisible and visible parts of Satan's world will be completely destroyed.[468]   Armageddon, the "war of the great day of God the Almighty" (Rev. 16:14),[469] will be a war in which the nations of the world will fight against God's kingdom headed by His Anointed One, Jesus[470]; it will be a battle between those who are for and those who are against Jehovah's universal sovereignty.[471] Jehovah will actually welcome this fight, for it will give Him the opportunity of vindicating His universal sovereignty over the earth.[472]

[463] *Make Sure of All Things*, p. 390. The astounding implication of these words is that Christ did not engage in actual combat with Satan previous to 1914, and that he does not do so between 1918 and Armageddon!

[464] *Ibid.*

[465] *Paradise Lost*, p. 210; *You May Survive Armageddon*, pp. 217, 347.

[466] "The unrighteous 'goats' will be everlastingly cut off from all life in the battle of Armageddon with which this old world will end" (*Paradise Lost*, p. 202).

[467] *Let God Be True*, pp. 260, 201. In the latter passage the role of Jehovah's Witnesses is compared to that of Noah before the flood.

[468] *Ibid.*, p. 259. This statement must not be taken entirely at face value, however, since Satan is only "abyssed" at Armageddon, to be loosed again at the end of the millennium.

[469] *Paradise Lost*, p. 203.

[470] *You May Survive Armageddon*, p. 333.

[471] *Ibid.*, p. 338.

[472] *Ibid.*, p. 334. Note the conception of the nature of Jehovah which underlies this statement!

Satan is now grouping his forces in preparation for the war of Armageddon.[473]   His demons are leading the nations to prepare to do battle against those who visibly represent the kingdom of God, the remnant and their companions in the New World Society.[474]

Where will this battle be fought?   Though the word *Armageddon,* or *Har-Magedon,* derived from Rev. 16:16, means "mountain of Megiddo," this battle will not be fought just at the field of Megiddo in Palestine since this battlefield would be too small to hold all the kings of the earth and their armies.[475] The battle will be fought in all quarters of the globe.[476] The reason why this battle is called that of Armageddon is that the battles fought in ancient times at Megiddo in Palestine were decisive: the armies that won there won complete victories, whereas those that lost suffered total defeat.[477]

When will this battle be fought?   At the close of the "time of the end," which will be very soon.[478]   It was affirmed in 1952 that this war would begin inside our generation.[479]   In a volume published in 1958 we are told that many people alive since 1914 will still be living when Armageddon begins.[480]

Just before Armageddon begins, the devil will attack the New World Society.[481]   This attack will provoke Jehovah to anger; He will then unleash the Battle of Armageddon by giving Christ the command to destroy the devil's wicked world.[482]   The invisible "appearance" of Christ at this time is called "the revelation of the Lord Jesus from heaven" depicted in II Thessalonians 1:7-10[483]; this revelation (*apokalupsis*) is distinguished from the second presence of Christ (*parousia*) which occurred in 1914.[484]   This

---

[473] *Let God Be True,* p. 259.
[474] *You May Survive Armageddon,* pp. 333-34.   At this point Rev. 12:17 is quoted, the same passage to which Seventh-day Adventists appeal to support their conception of the "remnant church."   Cf. *Paradise Lost,* p. 203, where a similar statement is made, buttressed by a reference to Rev. 16:14, 16.
[475] *Paradise Lost,* pp. 203-4.
[476] *You May Survive Armageddon,* p. 337.
[477] *Paradise Lost,* p. 203.
[478] *Ibid.,* p. 205.
[479] *Let God Be True,* p. 179.
[480] *Paradise Lost,* p. 205.
[481] *Ibid.,* p. 206.
[482] *Ibid.,* p. 207.
[483] *You May Survive Armageddon,* p. 27.
[484] *This Means Everlasting Life,* p. 222.

"appearance" of Christ on earth is called "the final revelation of the King"[485] and is even referred to as his "return."[486]

Who will be drawn up in battle array at the War of Armageddon? On the one side will be all the nations of the world, the members of the United Nations (the beast of Rev. 17), the religious heads of heathendom and Christendom (the woman who rides the beast), and all the goats that have been separated from the sheep by the judgment of the nations just concluded (this last group will include most of Christendom).[487] On the other side will be the remnant of spiritual Israel (that is, the members of the 144,000 left on earth at that time) and the "great crowd" of other sheep[488] — a crowd, however, which will look very small compared to the vast hordes which oppose them. In addition to these visible forces there will be invisible combatants as well. Fighting against God will be the devil and all the demons.[489] Fighting on the side of the remnant and the other sheep, however, will be Jesus Christ and, following his leadership, the unseen hosts of heaven (that is, the angels) together with those of his anointed followers who have been "resurrected."[490]

The remnant and the other sheep do not need to fight at Armageddon; Christ and his heavenly armies will do all the fighting for them.[491] When we ask what weapons will be used by the rebellious nations, we get an ambiguous answer. On the one hand we are told that the nations will use their military, naval, and air equipment,[492] and that they will release atomic bombs, hydro-

---

[485] *Let God Be True,* p. 205.

[486] *Ibid.,* p. 206. So there are two "returns" of Christ: the first one, which occurred in 1914, when he ascended the throne of his kingdom; and a second one, which will occur when he comes to earth to conduct the Battle of Armageddon! It is therefore not quite correct to say that Jehovah's Witnesses do not look for *any* future "return" of Christ. Even this future return, however, will be an invisible one (*ibid.,* p. 205).

[487] *You May Survive Armageddon,* p. 338; see above, pp. 43-44. It is evident from this description why Jehovah's Witnesses attack not only all churches but also all political organizations and governments. All governments and all churches are part of the devil's visible organization. The Witnesses therefore refuse to salute the flag of any nation since, so they say, such an act ascribes salvation to the nation for which the flag stands, and is an act of idolatry (*Let God Be True,* pp. 242-43).

[488] *You May Survive Armageddon,* pp. 338-39.

[489] *Paradise Lost,* p. 203.

[490] *You May Survive Armageddon,* pp. 338-39. The revelation of Christ at Armageddon will, however, be an invisible one. Thus neither Christ nor his heavenly armies will be seen by men.

[491] *Paradise Lost,* p. 204.

[492] *You May Survive Armageddon,* p. 337.

gen bombs, disease-germ bombs, and chemical gas bombs.[493] Yet on the other hand we are informed that the wood of the weapons of Gog's hordes (that is, those of the devil) will make so large a pile that it will take seven years to use it up as fuel. These weapons are then designated as follows: shields, bows and arrows, handstaves, and spears.[494] Jehovah, however, will completely exterminate His enemies by unleashing such terrors as cloudbursts, floods, earthquakes, hailstones, fires, and flesh-eating plagues.[495] The fire of Armageddon will, in fact, be far more destructive than literal fire; it will completely envelop the devil's visible and invisible organizations.[496]

The results of this terrible battle will be worse than those of any previous war in history. Over two billion people will die.[497] All of Christendom will be wiped out,[498] and all the nations will be destroyed.[499] "Satan's entire world or system of things, its invisible demonic heavens and its visible wicked human earth, will be destroyed. . . ."[500] Dead bodies will be everywhere, from one end of the earth to the other; these shall neither be wept over nor buried.[501] Not a single human being who was against Jehovah's organization will survive.[502]

Only faithful Jehovah's Witnesses — members of the remnant or of the other sheep — will survive Armageddon; these "will stand and see the salvation of Jehovah for them."[503] Jehovah will not allow His executioners to touch them.[504] These Armageddon survivors will be assigned the duty of gathering up the bones that are left of the slain, and of burying them (not the bodies; just the

---

[493] *Ibid.*, p. 340.
[494] *Ibid.*, p. 343.
[495] *Paradise Lost*, pp. 207-208.
[496] *New Heavens and a New Earth*, p. 294.
[497] *You May Survive Armageddon*, p. 341.
[498] *Ibid.*, p. 217.
[499] *Ibid.*, p. 57.
[500] *Ibid.*, p. 346.
[501] *Paradise Lost*, p. 210.
[502] *You May Survive Armageddon*, p. 342.
[503] *Ibid.*, p. 347. Note that what determines survival at Armageddon is not first of all faith in Jesus Christ as Saviour, but membership in the New World Society. Faith in the all-sufficient atonement of Christ will not save from total annihilation any member of "Christendom" unaffiliated with the Watchtower organization.
[504] *Ibid.*, p. 217. When we ask how anyone can be expected to live through this devastating holocaust, or how Jehovah's Witnesses will be kept safe from enemy bullets and bombs, we are told that "Jehovah will perform a stupendous miracle in preserving them [His people] through the terrifying destruction" (*This Means Everlasting Life*, p. 266).

bleached bones).[505]   The survivors are also given the task of converting whatever instruments of combat are left on the earth into implements of peace.[506]

To complete the story of the Battle of Armageddon, it should be mentioned that, at the end of the battle, Satan and his demons are cast into the "abyss" by Christ, who is said to be the angel referred to in Revelation 20:1.[507] The abyss is not a symbol for the condition of nonexistence; it stands for a deathlike state of inactivity.[508]   Thus, both the devil and his demons having been rendered inactive, the world is ready for the millennium which now begins.

The Millennium. Jehovah's Witnesses understand the thousand years of Revelation 20 as pointing to a literal thousand-year period, beginning immediately after Armageddon, during which God's new world is to be established on earth.   This period is referred to in their literature as that of Christ's millennial reign,[509] or of his thousand-year reign.[510]   God's new world is said to consist of "new heavens and a new earth." By the new heavens the Witnesses understand "the righteous new heavenly ruling powers, Christ Jesus with his 'bride' of 144,000 members."[511] By the new earth they mean "not a new earthly globe, but the righteous earthly subjects of the King living under a new social arrangement."[512]

This leads us to consider the role of the 144,000 during the millennium.   They are, of course, not on earth but in heaven (except for those few still living on earth after Armageddon,

---

[505] *Paradise Lost,* p. 211.
[506] *The Truth Shall Make You Free,* p. 360.
[507] *Paradise Lost,* p. 211.
[508] *Ibid.*
[509] *New Heavens and a New Earth,* p. 321.
[510] *Paradise Lost,* p. 226.   At this point a question arises: Since Christ began ruling from his heavenly throne in 1914, why is this period referred to as "the thousand years of Christ's reign" (*Let God Be True,* p. 270)? And how can the 144,000 be said to reign a thousand years with Christ during the millennium (*ibid.,* p. 137), when they actually began to reign with him in 1918?
[511] *Religion for Mankind,* p. 377.   Actually, the new heavens in this sense began to come into existence in 1918, when the first group of anointed ones began to be "raised"; these new heavens, further, are not complete until some time after the millennium has begun since there will still be members of the remnant living on earth after Armageddon.
[512] *Ibid.*   It will be recalled that in the Battle of Armageddon Satan's demonic heavens and wicked human earth were destroyed (see above, p. 105).

who will join the heavenly assembly as soon as they die).[513] The 144,000 in heaven are, during the millennium, the invisible part of the new world,[514] the ruling body of Jehovah's universal organization.[515] In the capacity of priests and kings they reign with Christ during the millennium.[516] They may therefore be called "associate kings" and "royal priests"[517]; since the power of judging has also been bestowed upon them,[518] they may in addition be called "associate judges."[519] It may be gathered from the above that the 144,000 will therefore help Christ in carrying out his kingly, priestly, and judicial activities. We are told, in fact, that they "join him [Christ] in dispensing the benefits of Christ's ransom sacrifice to the believers of mankind during the thousand years of the Kingdom rule."[520] We are further informed that they must officiate as priests "for the everlasting good of mankind, even to bringing back all the dead who are in the graves."[521] Christ, in fact, will not even be able to bring the inhabitants of God's new world to perfection without the help of his heavenly bride:

> The ministry of the heavenly High Priest together with the 144,000 who will be his underpriests and "priests of God" will lift up the antitypical twelve tribes of Israel to human perfection by the end of the thousand years of Christ's reign.[522]

What will the earth be like during the millennium? The earth, it is said, will be cleansed after Armageddon.[523] Soon after the devastation of Armageddon has been removed, the earth will become a new paradise, replacing the paradise lost at the dawn of history.[524] The whole earth will be made into a garden; under

[513] *New Heavens and a New Earth,* p. 321; *You May Survive Armageddon,* p. 352.
[514] *Let God Be True,* p. 138.
[515] *Ibid.,* p. 130.
[516] *Ibid.,* p. 137.
[517] *This Means Everlasting Life,* p. 275.
[518] *You May Survive Armageddon,* p. 276.
[519] *Make Sure of All Things,* p. 221.
[520] *This Means Everlasting Life,* pp. 274-75. Christ therefore needs the services of the 144,000 in applying the fruits of his atonement to his people.
[521] *Ibid.,* p. 275. Apparently Christ cannot raise the dead without the help of the 144,000.
[522] *You May Survive Armageddon,* p. 353.
[523] *Paradise Lost,* p. 216. Yet this cleansing is not final. For, on p. 239 of the same volume, we are told that it is not until the execution of judgment over Satan and his followers at the end of the millennium that the perfect earth will be cleansed.
[524] *Ibid.,* pp. 220ff.

Jehovah's direction, aided by an ideal climate and the absence of destructive pests, the survivors of Armageddon will replant the earthly paradise.[525]   Man will again subdue the earth and have dominion over the lower creation; all the beasts will now be at peace with each other and with man.[526]   On this new earth there will be neither thorns nor thistles.[527]   There will be no more famine or drought; no diseases, aches, or pains; and no more old age, since perpetual youth will be the lot of all the faithful.[528] Death will also be largely eliminated[529] — the only ones who will die during the millennium will be those members of the remnant that survived Armageddon and those inhabitants of the new earth who refuse to obey Jehovah (these as we shall see, will be annihilated).   All results of sin in human social life will also have been removed.   There will be no more war, no crime, no lawlessness or vice — since all people who want to do bad things have been killed at Armageddon.[530]   Hence there will be no need for armed troops or for police forces.[531]   All will be at peace with each other since all will be united in the worship of the one true God.[532]

During the millennium the earth, which was denuded of all human inhabitants except Jehovah's Witnesses by the Battle of Armageddon, will be repopulated.   How will this repopulation take place?   First, by the birth of children to the Armageddon survivors, and, second, by a series of resurrections.   Let us look at each of these methods in detail.

Children Born During the Millennium.   Children will be born to the survivors of Armageddon.[533]   These Armageddon survivors may expect to receive a mandate from God through Christ enjoining them to reproduce their kind.[534] Since not all of these survivors were married when Armageddon came, there will be marriages during the millennium.[535] Because children so born will not die — unless they prove rebellious — and because room must be

[525] *Ibid.,* p. 221.
[526] *Let God Be True,* p. 267.
[527] *New Heavens and a New Earth,* p. 344.
[528] *Let God Be True,* pp. 267-68.
[529] *Ibid.,* p. 268.
[530] *Ibid.,* p. 267; *Paradise Lost,* pp. 221-22.
[531] *Let God Be True,* p. 267.
[532] *Ibid.,* p. 266.
[533] *You May Survive Armageddon,* p. 351.
[534] *New Heavens and a New Earth,* pp. 331-32.
[535] *Let God Be True,* p. 269.

left on the earth for those who will be raised from the dead, God
will see to it that, at a certain point of time, childbearing will
cease.[536]

A word should be said about the nature of these children.
Infant death, needless to say, will no longer occur during the
millennium; neither will any of these children be cripples.[537] Yet
they will not be perfect; "being born of not yet perfect although
righteous parents,[538] these children will not be born any more
perfect than their parents then."[539] Though imperfect, the children
born to Armageddon survivors will not grow older, however, nor
weaker and impaired with age, but will grow "young, strong, and
gradually freed from all blemishes and marks of imperfection."[540]
Their parents will teach them to do right, transmitting to them
God's instructions. Though Godfearing parents before the
millennium train their children in an imperfect way, during the
millennium parents will be able to perform this task "in a
perfect and complete way under God's direction."[541]

Resurrections During the Millennium. Before discussing the
various groups that will be raised during the millennium, we should
examine the nature of these resurrections. According to Jehovah-
Witness teaching, there is no soul which survives after death. When
a man dies he totally ceases to exist.[542] Yet the Witnesses do
teach that people will be "raised" from the dead. We have already
looked at their teaching on the so-called first or nonphysical
"resurrection" which the members of the anointed class experience.
There are others, however — their number will far exceed that

[536] *Paradise Lost,* p. 225. There appears to be some ambiguity in
Jehovah-Witness teaching on the question of whether only Armageddon
survivors will be able to bring forth children during the millennium,
or whether this privilege will be extended also to the other sheep raised
from the dead after Armageddon. On pp. 362-64 of *The Truth Shall
Make You Free* (published in 1943) we are told that the other sheep
raised after Armageddon will have a part in fulfilling the divine mandate
to bring forth children. In later publications, however, it is said that
only Armageddon survivors will have this privilege (*Let God Be True,*
pp. 268-69; *Paradise Lost,* pp. 224, 226). Perhaps there has been a shift
in Watchtower thinking on this point.
[537] *Paradise Lost,* p. 225.
[538] A strange combination, to say the least!
[539] *New Heavens and a New Earth,* p. 346.
[540] *You May Survive Armageddon,* p. 353.
[541] *Paradise Lost,* pp. 224-25. Another strange combination: parents
who are still imperfect will be able, during the millennium, to do a perfect
job of training their children!
[542] See above, pp. 85-87.

of 144,000 — who will be raised with physical bodies. Yet even these resurrections with physical bodies are not, strictly speaking, resurrections. Since these individuals were totally annihilated when they died, it would be more accurate to call the "resurrections" which are now said to occur *new creations*.[543] Interestingly enough, Watchtower authors even use the word *create* to describe this type of resurrection: "through Jesus Christ who died for them [people to be raised during the millennium], God will create new bodies for them."[544]

This type of resurrection is described as a "reactivating of the life pattern of the creature."[545] This is possible only because the life pattern of every creature to be so raised is on record with God. God therefore re-creates these individuals on the basis of His memory of what they were like before they died.[546] "People who have been kept in God's memory will be brought back to life from their death state to enjoy the benefits of God's righteous new world."[547] A human being so raised will retain his personal identity "by the setting in motion again of the distinctive life pattern of that individual."[548] Such a person will have the same personality that he had when he died; he will therefore be recognizable by acquaintances.[549]

It should be noted that those who are physically raised during the millennium are not raised with perfect human bodies. Their

---

[543] See the comment made about the Seventh-day Adventist conception of the resurrection in *The Four Major Cults*, p. 140.

[544] *Paradise Lost*, p. 234.

[545] *Make Sure of All Things*, p. 311 (see above, pp. 95-96, where this rather detailed description is quoted in full).

[546] *Ibid.*

[547] *Paradise Lost*, p. 227. The implication is that some have not been kept in God's memory and will therefore not be brought back to life. This point is made explicit on p. 364 of *The Truth Shall Make You Free*. Here, speaking of people who are cast into Gehenna, the place of final destruction, the authors say, ". . . They are not spoken of as 'in the tombs' or 'in the graves,' which is to say, in the memory of God as having an opportunity for redemption by Christ's blood. . . . God will not remember them in the time of 'resurrection of the dead, both of the just and unjust.' "

[548] *Make Sure of All Things*, p. 311.

[549] *Survival After Death*, p. 38. It is significant that, for the Witnesses, a resurrection with a physical body is of lower value than one with a nonphysical body, since the latter is experienced only by Christ and the 144,000, whereas the former is experienced by the more numerous other sheep. Again we see in Watchtower teaching a kind of Gnostic disparagement of the physical body.

new bodies, it is said, will match the personalities of the individuals who are raised — personalities which were neither sinless nor perfect at the moment of death.[550] These individuals, therefore, are raised in a fallen condition; only by the end of the millennium will they have been lifted out of their fallen condition and brought to a condition of human perfection.[551]

A great number of people will be raised with physical bodies during the millennium. One statement, in fact, gives the impression that most people who have ever lived will be so raised: "The greater mass of humankind will find life here on earth amid paradise conditions."[552] There will be some, however, who will not be brought back from death. Christ himself will judge who deserve to be raised or who could profit from being raised.[553]

Those Not Raised During the Millennium. Let us now note which individuals will not be raised from the dead. As we have previously observed, none of those killed at Armageddon will be raised. All those who knowingly and deliberately did wrong will not be raised.[554] Those who died wicked beyond reform or correction and beyond redemption by Christ's blood will not be raised.[555] This group includes all who have sinned against the holy spirit.[556] Among those included in the number of people who will not be raised are Adam and Eve[557]; it is said that, since

[550] *Paradise Lost,* p. 234.
[551] *Ibid.,* p. 238; *Let God Be True,* p. 293. At the beginning of the millennium, therefore, all three groups that make up the population of the new earth are still imperfect: the Armageddon survivors, the children born to them, and those raised from the dead. Gradually, however, as the millennium progresses, they advance toward perfection, through the ministry of the heavenly High Priest and the 144,000 (*You May Survive Armageddon,* p. 353). This perfecting does not take place without the obedient cooperation of millennial mankind with Christ during the thousand years (*This Means Everlasting Life,* p. 304).
[552] *Let God Be True,* p. 279. Jehovah's Witnesses are not universalists, since they teach that some will be annihilated. Yet the above statement suggests that, in their judgment, the number of those annihilated will be small in comparison with the number of the saved.
[553] *You May Survive Armageddon,* p. 354. The statement "who could profit from being raised" is puzzling, in view of the fact that some who are raised during the millennium will disobey God and consequently be annihilated. Did these individuals really "profit" from their resurrection? Could not Christ have foreseen their disobedience and simply have left them in the condition of nonexistence in which they were before their resurrection?
[554] *Paradise Lost,* p. 229.
[555] *Let God Be True,* p. 289.
[556] *Ibid.* How can one, however, sin against an impersonal force?
[557] *Paradise Lost,* p. 236.

Adam had his final judgment in the garden of Eden, and was sentenced there, he will not be raised for any further judgment during the millennium.[558]   Others who will not be raised include Cain,[559] those who died in the flood, the people of Sodom,[560] Judas Iscariot, and the religious hypocrites of Jesus' day.[561]   All these will simply be left in the nonexistence into which death has plunged them.

The "Resurrection of Life."   Jehovah's Witnesses distinguish between two kinds of resurrection during the millennium: a "resurrection of life" and a "resurrection of judgment."   They base this distinction on the words of Jesus recorded in John 5:28-29: ". . . the hour is coming in which all those in the memorial tombs will hear his voice and come out, those who did good things to a resurrection of life, those who practiced vile things to a resurrection of judgment" (NWT).   The "resurrection of life" includes the resurrection of faithful men of God who lived before Pentecost, and of other sheep who died before Armageddon.[562]   The "resurrection of judgment" is that of the rest of mankind who have not been judged worthy of being destroyed.[563]

The "resurrection of life" includes, first, that of Old Testament people who were faithful to God and that of others who lived at the time of Christ but died before Pentecost.[564]   "These men knew that their hope was in a resurrection to life right here on earth.   And they really had strong faith in the fact that they would be resurrected."[565]   When these ancient worthies are raised, they will become "other sheep" of the Right Shepherd.[566]

Many of these Old Testament saints will be made theocratic

---

[558] *Let God Be True*, p. 289.   It is striking to note the difference between the view of Adam held by Mormons and Jehovah's Witnesses.   By the latter, he is not even considered worthy of being raised from the dead; by the former, however, he is hailed as one of the noblest characters that ever lived and is even looked upon as a god! (*The Four Major Cults*, pp. 41, 51).

[559] *You May Survive Armageddon*, p. 354.

[560] *Paradise Lost*, p. 236.

[561] *You May Survive Armageddon*, p. 354.

[562] *Paradise Lost*, p. 228.   On p. 231 it is said that the resurrection of the 144,000 was also part of the "resurrection of life."

[563] *Ibid.*, p. 229.

[564] *You May Survive Armageddon*, p. 355.

[565] *Paradise Lost*, p. 228.

[566] *You May Survive Armageddon*, p. 355.   They cannot become members of the 144,000 because they died before Pentecost, when the anointed class began to be gathered.

princes — that is, will be given princely or leading positions in the new earth, as the visible representatives of Christ.[567]   Among these will be Enoch, Noah, Abraham, Isaac, Jacob, David,[568] Moses, and Daniel.[569]   However, some of the other sheep who have survived Armageddon will also be made princes[570]; since many of them occupy positions as theocratic princes in the New World Society today, before Armageddon, they will carry these princely responsibilities with them through Armageddon.[571]   Thus the inhabitants of the new earth will be given good rulers, chosen for this purpose by Jesus Christ himself.[572]

Since those who are to be made princes must serve as rulers of the new earth, they will be raised first.[573]   The next group to be raised, also as part of the "resurrection of life," will be the other sheep who died before Armageddon.[574]   These, though unable to share the heavenly blessedness of the 144,000, will be able to enjoy everlasting life on the paradise earth if they remain faithful to God.[575]   Though Jesus expressly said that they would inherit the kingdom prepared for them (Mt. 25:34), we are given to understand that this is not the kingdom of heaven but the earthly realm of the kingdom of heaven.[576]

The "Resurrection of Judgment."   After the princes and the other sheep have been raised, there follows the "resurrection of judgment."[577]   This is the resurrection of people "whose hearts may have been wanting to do right, but who died without ever having had an opportunity to hear of God's purposes or to learn what He expects of men."[578]   These individuals are further described as having been sincere in their belief, but having lacked an opportunity to learn of righteousness from God.   This opportunity they will now receive.[579]   This group will include the peni-

---

[567] *Ibid.*, p. 355.
[568] *Ibid.*
[569] *Religion for Mankind*, p. 339.
[570] *Let God Be True*, pp. 139, 263.
[571] *You May Survive Armageddon*, pp. 355-56.
[572] *Paradise Lost*, p. 218.
[573] *Ibid.*, p. 232.
[574] *Ibid.*
[575] *Let God Be True*, p. 282.
[576] *Paradise Lost*, p. 202.
[577] *Ibid.*, p. 233.
[578] *Ibid.*, p. 229.
[579] *Ibid.*

tent thief.[580]   Along with him, billions of others will be brought back for this "resurrection of judgment."[581]   These resurrections will be spread out over a long period so that people who have been raised earlier can help to get things ready for those who are yet to return.[582]

After this "resurrection of judgment" has begun, an ambitious educational program will be inaugurated. Those now raised from the dead must be taught the truth and shown what is right.[583] An extensive educational work will therefore be necessary to give instruction in God's law to these unrighteous dead as they arise from their tombs.[584]   During the millennium they will be learning righteousness from the Judge and through his earthly princes.[585]

The Day of Judgment. Jehovah's Witnesses speak of a "Judgment Day" for mankind; this day, however, is not to be a twenty-four-hour day but is to extend through the first thousand years of the new world.[586] ' The inhabited earth which, according to Paul's words in Acts 17:31, is to be judged by Christ is not the present world (which has been judged and condemned at Armageddon), but the world to come, that is, the inhabited earth as it exists during the millennium.[587]   Anyone not inhabiting the earth in the new world will therefore not be involved in this judgment.[588] All those who will be on earth during the millennium, however, will be involved in this judgment,[589] which is also called a thousand-year day of test.[590]

The basis for this judgment will not be the lives people have lived before they died, but the works they perform during the mil-

---

[580] *Ibid.*   To justify their position, the authors punctuate Lk. 23:43 as follows: "Verily I say unto thee this day. With me shalt thou be in Paradise."

[581] *Ibid.*, p. 232.

[582] *Ibid.*

[583] *Ibid.*, p. 229.

[584] *Let God Be True*, p. 270.

[585] *Ibid.*, p. 293.   Note that nothing is said in this connection about the atoning work of Jesus Christ. The emphasis is all on doing right and learning God's laws!   Christ's ransom has provided the basis for their resurrection from the dead, but their acquisition of everlasting life is dependent solely on their obedience to God's laws.

[586] *Ibid.*, p. 286.   For proof the authors quote II Peter 3:8, "one day is with the Lord as a thousand years, and a thousand years as one day."

[587] *Ibid.*, pp. 285-86.

[588] *Ibid.*, p. 286.

[589] *Ibid.*, p. 288.

[590] *Make Sure of All Things*, p. 224.

lennium.[591]   Armageddon survivors will be judged according to
their faithfulness to God and Christ throughout the thousand-year
judgment day; if they are approved, they will receive the right to
eternal life.[592]   Children born of Armageddon survivors will have
full opportunity for life through Christ the King; they will also be
judged on the basis of their works — any of them not desiring
to serve Jehovah will be executed.[593] All those raised from the
dead during the millennium will likewise be judged.   Those raised
in the "resurrection of judgment" will be judged according to what
they do with the training they now receive; if they obey God's
commands, they will get everlasting life; but if they do not obey,
they will go into everlasting death.[594]

> Jesus Christ the Right Shepherd died for them [those raised
> in the "resurrection of judgment"] not to put them on judgment
> for their past vile lives, but to provide for them a period of
> judgment in the new world in hope of their reforming and prac-
> ticing good things and deserving to be lifted up to human per-
> fection, thus to be judged according to their future works under
> the Kingdom.   They will have the opportunity to become "other
> sheep" by listening to the voice of the Shepherd King and
> obediently following him, that he may gather them into the "one
> flock."[595]

In the case of some this judgment will result in annihilation.
Those who refuse to obey God's kingdom, after a long enough
trial, will be sentenced to everlasting destruction [annihilation] before the end of the millennium.[596]   Risen ones who prove unre-
formable or turn rebellious will be executed.[597]   The vast majority,
however, will pass the judgment-test and receive everlasting life
on the new earth.[598]

We see therefore that, according to Jehovah-Witness teaching,
most of the inhabitants of the earth will have a second opportunity
to make life's most momentous decision after they have died. The

[591] *Ibid.*, p. 225; *Let God Be True*, p. 293.
[592] *Let God Be True*, p. 290.
[593] *Ibid.*, p. 269.
[594] *Paradise Lost*, p. 229.
[595] *You May Survive Armageddon*, p. 356.   Note once again that the
ultimate basis for the salvation of these individuals is not the work of
Christ for them but their "reforming and practicing good things."   This is
not salvation by grace but salvation by works!
[596] *Paradise Lost*, p. 237.
[597] *You May Survive Armageddon*, pp. 356-57.
[598] *Let God Be True*, p. 279.

Watchtower conception of the judgment day is radically different from that of historic Christianity since, as we have seen, the judgment is based, for them, not on deeds done in this life but on what is done during the millennium.[599]

Satan's Final Battle. Though the "Day of Judgment" extends throughout the millennium, this is still not the last judgment; "the final judgment will not come until the end of Christ's thousand-year reign."[600] At this point the King, Jesus Christ, steps aside to allow the Supreme Judge, Jehovah, to make the final test.[601] This last test or judgment will occur by means of Satan's final battle. At the end of the millennium Satan and his demons will be loosed or released from the abyss in which they have been confined for a thousand years.[602] Satan, his mental attitude unchanged, will once again seek to usurp Jehovah's position of sovereignty over the universe, and will once again try to turn mankind against God.[603] He will use some sly appeal to selfishness, making people think they will be better off if they follow him.[604] This attempt of Satan will be a final test of obedience which everyone on earth will have to face — even the princes and the Armageddon survivors.[605] The human race which thus faces its final trial is, it must be remembered, a perfected one.[606]

Sad to say, however, some of earth's perfected inhabitants will be led astray by Satan and will join him.[607] Satan, his demons, and his followers now assault the "camp of the holy ones," made up

---

[599] At this point we may well ask whether the Battle of Armageddon is really a revelation of God's justice, as the Witnesses claim. For is it not true that many of those killed in this battle have not had an opportunity to hear God's purposes or to learn what He expects of men? In the case of millions of these Armageddon victims, if they had happened to die one week — or, for that matter, one day — before Armageddon, they would have been among those raised in the "resurrection of judgment," and given a new opportunity to learn about God's kingdom. But, because they happened to have the misfortune of living at the time of Armageddon, they were put to death without any hope of resurrection. Is this divine "justice"?

[600] *Paradise Lost,* pp. 237-38.

[601] *New Heavens and a New Earth,* p. 353.

[602] *Let God Be True,* pp. 270, 293.

[603] *Ibid.,* p. 270.

[604] *Paradise Lost,* p. 239.

[605] *Ibid.,* p. 238.

[606] *You May Survive Armageddon,* p. 357.

[607] *Let God Be True,* p. 270; *New Heavens and a New Earth,* p. 354. Another strange phenomenon! Earlier we saw that imperfect parents will be able during the millennium to do a perfect job of training their children (above, p. 109). Now we observe that perfect people can still be led astray by Satan and can still rebel against God!

of perfect humanity, and the "beloved city," challenging Jehovah's sovereignty for the last time.[608]   Fire comes down out of heaven, however, and devours all those who follow Satan.[609]   All human rebels, all the demons, and Satan himself will now be cast into the lake of fire and sulphur, which stands for everlasting destruction.[610] All these will be consigned to the "second death," which means annihilation.[611]   They will be as if they had never existed; "their cursed name will rot."[612]

Those who do not yield to Satan's temptation, however, and who thus pass this final test, will be declared righteous by Jehovah,[613] and will be given the right to perfect life on the paradise earth forever.[614]   Thus the inhabitants of the new world will receive what Adam lost long ago: everlasting life on a paradise earth.[615]   The earth has now been finally cleansed, since everyone who would disobey Jehovah has been annihilated, and everyone who remains will have proved that he intends to obey God forever.[616]   The great controversy that has raged throughout the universe is now settled[617]; Jehovah's sovereignty has now been ultimately vindicated!

The Final State.   As has already been implied, Jehovah's Witnesses repudiate the doctrine of eternal torment for the finally impenitent, claiming that this doctrine is based on Satan's original lie in Eden.[618]   They advance four reasons why this doctrine is to be rejected: (1) it is wholly unscriptural; (2) it is unreasonable; (3) it is contrary to God's love; and (4) it is repugnant to justice.[619]

In this connection we should briefly examine Watchtower teachings about Gehenna, the New Testament word usually rendered *hell* in our English translations.   In a note found on pages 766-67 of their *New World Translation of the Christian Greek*

[608] *New Heavens and a New Earth,* p. 354.
[609] *Paradise Lost,* p. 239.
[610] *Let God Be True,* p. 270.
[611] *Ibid.,* p. 293.
[612] *New Heavens and a New Earth,* p. 355.
[613] This is the final justification of the other sheep alluded to in n. 317, above.   Remember that this is a justification based on works rather than on faith.
[614] *Paradise Lost,* p. 240; *Let God Be True,* pp. 280, 293.
[615] *Paradise Lost,* p. 234.
[616] *Ibid.,* p. 239.
[617] *New Heavens and a New Earth,* p. 351.
[618] *Make Sure of All Things,* p. 155.
[619] *Let God Be True,* p. 99.

Scriptures, the authors explain that the word Gehenna is the Greek form of the Hebrew *Gei-Hinnom,* which means "valley of Hinnom." This valley, which lay west and south of ancient Jerusalem, came to be the dumping place and incinerator for the filth of the city. Fires were kept burning there continually. The bodies of dead animals or of executed criminals were sometimes thrown into this valley; occasionally these bodies landed on a ledge, in which case they were devoured by worms which did not die until they had consumed the fleshy parts. No living animals were ever thrown into Gehenna. Hence, it is said, this place could never symbolize a region where human souls are "tormented in literal fire and attacked by undying immortal worms for ever and ever."

> Because the dead criminals cast here were denied a decent burial in a memorial tomb, which symbolizes the hope of a resurrection, Gehenna was used by Jesus and his disciples to symbolize everlasting destruction, annihilation from God's universe, or "second death," an eternal punishment.[620]

The word Hades, as we have seen,[621] is interpreted to mean simply the grave. A further refinement is added to the definition of Hades, however, on page 155 of *Make Sure of All Things:*

> After Jesus introduced the truth about life and immortality, only the willfully wicked were spoken of as being in Gehenna, the expression *Hades* [translated "hell" in English] being applied to the dead in God's memory, those with opportunity or hope of a resurrection.

Gehenna, therefore, is for Jehovah's Witnesses a symbol of annihilation — an annihilation from which there is no awakening,[622] and no resurrection.[623] People who are cast into Gehenna do not remain in the memory of God.[624] Gehenna, "the second death," and "the lake that burneth with fire and brimstone" all stand for the same thing: total annihilation.[625] Such total annihilation is therefore the doom of the "goats" at the Battle of Armageddon[626]; of all those who will not be raised during the millennium; of all those who, though living on the new earth during the millennium,

---

[620] P. 767. Cf. *Let God Be True,* pp. 95-96; *Make Sure of All Things,* p. 155.
[621] Above, p. 86.
[622] *Make Sure of All Things,* p. 155.
[623] *Let God Be True,* p. 96.
[624] *The Truth Shall Make You Free,* p. 364.
[625] *Ibid.*
[626] *Let God Be True,* p. 97.

refuse to obey God's kingdom[627]; and of all who follow Satan in his final battle.[628]

Jehovah's Witnesses, however, do not claim to be denying the doctrine of eternal punishment; they insist that total annihilation *is* eternal punishment since it is total, final, and therefore eternal destruction. The authors of *Let God Be True* render the first part of Matthew 25:46 as follows: "These [the 'goats'] will depart into everlasting cutting-off [Greek, *kolasis*]. . . ," adding the comment, "So the everlasting punishment of the 'goats' is their everlastingly being cut off from all life."[629]

We see, therefore, that in the final state all who have rebelled against Jehovah and have refused to obey the laws of His kingdom will have been annihilated, and that only those members of the human race and of the angelic hosts who have proved loyal to Jehovah are still in existence. Let us now note what Jehovah's Witnesses teach about each of these remaining groups.

The other sheep, including all who were raised during the millennium and have passed the millennial tests, will remain forever on the renewed earth.[630] These other sheep are not given immortality, but will continue to exist everlastingly, though still dependent on food.[631] No other creature in the universe can now cause their death. "It is in this sense that these loyal ones gain the endless world to come and can never die any more."[632] It must be remembered, however, that the "second death" is always

---

[627] *Paradise Lost*, p. 237; *You May Survive Armageddon*, p. 356.

[628] *Let God Be True*, p. 270.

[629] P. 97. This passage, as well as the entire question of the denial of eternal torment, is further discussed in Appendix E of *The Four Major Cults*. Note that, in this interpretation, no room is left for any gradation in the punishment of the finally impenitent — a gradation which is clearly called for by Lk. 12:47-48. Cf. the position of the Seventh-day Adventists on this matter (*The Four Major Cults*, p. 142).

[630] This is taught despite the fact that in Rev. 7:9 the "great crowd" is pictured as standing "before the throne and before the Lamb," and that in verse 15 we are told that the members of the great crowd "are rendering him [God] sacred service day and night in his temple" (NWT). The Witnesses also teach, however, that the throne of God is in heaven rather than on earth (*New Heavens and a New Earth*, p. 16), and that the Lamb is now in heaven (above, pp. 90-91). They further teach that the temple at which the 144,000 have been united with Christ is in heaven (*Let God Be True*, p. 132). What Biblical basis, then, do Jehovah's Witnesses have for insisting that the "great crowd" of other sheep never gets to heaven but remains eternally upon the earth?

[631] *Make Sure of All Things*, p. 243.

[632] *This Means Everlasting Life*, p. 305.

within God's power to administer to possible rebels.[633] God does not intend to transport these other sheep to different planets or to heaven; He will keep them on the earth as expert gardeners to maintain it as a glorious paradise.[634] This earth will never come to a flaming end, as some scientists predict, but will endure forever.[635]

From this new earth all illness, sorrow, tears, and religious confusion will have been abolished.[636] All men will obey God's commands.[637] The purpose of life on this new earth will be the worship and praise of God and the unselfish service of man.[638] Love will therefore prevail: "love first to God with all one's heart, mind, soul, and strength, and love for one's perfect, godly neighbor as for oneself."[639] Everyone will be eternally happy in the paradise of the new earth.[640]

What about the 144,000? The "resurrection" of the last of the 144,000, which has occurred during the millennium, will have completed the marriage of Christ, the Lamb of God, to his bride.[641] It will be recalled that only the 144,000 and Christ are given immortality, which is defined as follows: "Deathlessness, that is, the life principle of the person possessing it cannot be taken away."[642] The 144,000 remain in heaven throughout eternity; they never come down again to inhabit the earth.[643] They continue to reign with Christ as his joint-heirs and co-rulers in Jehovah's glorious theocracy.[644] The heavenly kingdom, consisting of Christ and the "resurrected" 144,000, remains forever as the invisible or heavenly

---

[633] *New Heavens and a New Earth*, p. 356; cf. *This Means Everlasting Life*, p. 303. So there exists the possibility that even these finally perfected inhabitants of the earth may still rebel against God! The above statement, however, does not seem to agree with what we find on pp. 239-40 of *Paradise Lost*: ". . . We can be sure that, when he [Jehovah] says that everyone who is living on earth is worthy of life [after the final test], never again will there be even a single case of rebellion or disobedience against him anywhere on earth!"

[634] *New Heavens and a New Earth*, p. 360.
[635] *Ibid.*, pp. 356-67.
[636] *Let God Be True*, p. 271.
[637] *Paradise Lost*, p. 240.
[638] *New Heavens and a New Earth*, p. 361.
[639] *You May Survive Armageddon*, p. 361.
[640] *New Heavens and a New Earth*, p. 360.
[641] *Ibid.*, p. 322.
[642] *Make Sure of All Things*, p. 243.
[643] *Let God Be True*, p. 132. On the legitimacy of the view that the anointed class remains eternally in heaven while the other sheep are on the earth, see above, pp. 82-83.
[644] *Let God Be True*, p. 132.

part of the new world.[645]   This kingdom will bring unheard-of increase of blessings throughout eternity.[646]

A word should be said about the continued existence of the angels.   The sentence of death pronounced upon the devil in paradise proves that "holy angels, such as Satan had been up till his rebellion, are not immortal, indestructible, but their living forever is hinged upon their perfect obedience to God."[647]   Theoretically, therefore, the holy angels can still be annihilated by God, since it is possible that they may become disobedient.   Since angels are not immortal, they must be sustained by food.[648]

We may summarize the Jehovah-Witness conception of the final state in their own words:

> Forever the new earth and the new heavens will remain in tune in the unifying worship of the only true God and in the unswerving love of righteousness.   Perfect mankind's home and its radiant sun and silvery moon will endure as long as God's kingdom by Christ Jesus, the great Son and Seed of David, and that is forever.[649]

[645] *Ibid.*, p. 138.
[646] *Make Sure of All Things*, p. 233.
[647] *Survival After Death*, p. 62.
[648] *Make Sure of All Things*, pp. 247 and 243.   See above, pp. 57-58.   We are not told what this food is.
[649] *New Heavens and a New Earth*, p. 356.

IV. Appendix: Jehovah-Witness Teaching on the Person of Christ

In the preceding chapter the teachings of Jehovah's Witnesses about the person of Christ have been set forth. In this appendix these teachings will be critically evaluated. It is important that we do this, since the confession of the full deity of Jesus Christ and of His equality with God the Father has always been one of the distinguishing marks of Christianity.

A Revival of Arianism

A bit of historical orientation will first be in order. Essentially, the Jehovah-Witness view of the person of Christ is a revival of the Arian heresy of the fourth century A.D. Arius (who lived from approximately A.D. 280 to 336) and his followers (called Arians) taught that the Son, whom they also called the Logos or Word, had a beginning, that the term *beget* when applied to the generation of the Son meant to *make,* and that therefore the Son was not of the same substance as the Father but was a creature who had been called into existence by the Father.[1] The Arians taught that there was a time when God was alone and was not yet a Father.[2] Arius went on to ascribe to Christ only a subordinate, secondary, created divinity.[3] He asserted that such titles as *God* or *Son of*

---

[1] J. N. D. Kelly, *Early Christian Doctrines* (London: Adam & Chas. Black, 1958), pp. 227-28.
[2] Reinhold Seeberg, *Textbook of the History of Doctrines,* trans. Chas. Hay (Grand Rapids: Baker, 1954), I, 203.
[3] D. S. Schaff, "Arianism," in *The New Schaff-Herzog Encyclopedia of Religious Knowledge* (Grand Rapids: Baker, reprinted 1960), I, 281.

God when applied to Christ were mere courtesy titles: " 'Even if He is called God,' wrote Arius, 'He is not God truly, but by participation in grace. . . . He too is called God in name only.' "[4] Up to this point, there is virtual identity between the teachings of Arius and those of present-day Jehovah's Witnesses on the person of Christ.

It should be borne in mind, however, that there are also differences between Arian teachings and those of the Watchtower. Among these differences the following may be mentioned: Arius and the Arians taught that Christ, the created being through whom God made the world, did in the course of time assume a human body, though this was a human body without a rational soul.[5] Thus Arius would not agree with Jehovah's Witnesses that Christ, who was a created angel, became a mere man and ceased to be an angel while he was on earth. Arius held that Christ continued to be the Logos during his stay on earth but assumed a human body and directed its activities; the Logos thus took the place of the human soul in the being which resulted from this union. Arius would therefore repudiate the discontinuity between Christ's prehuman and human stages which is implicit in Jehovah-Witness Christology. Further, Arius did not deny the personality of the Holy Spirit. He taught that the Holy Spirit was an "hypostasis" or person, but that his essence was utterly unlike that of the Son. The later Arians amplified this thought so as to teach that the Holy Spirit was the noblest of the creatures produced by the Son at the Father's bidding.[6] While denying the deity of the Holy Spirit, therefore, the Arians did not deny His personality, as Jehovah's Witnesses do.[7]

On the basic question, however, of the equality of the Son to the Father, the Witnesses take the Arian position: the Son is not equal to the Father but was created by the Father at a point in time. As is well known, the church rejected the Arian position at the Council of Nicaea in A.D. 325. The Nicene Creed, drafted by this council and accepted universally by Christians today, made the following affirmation about the deity of Christ:

[4] Kelly, *op. cit.,* p. 229. The quotation is from Athanasius' *Contra Arianos,* I, 6.

[5] Kelly, *op. cit.,* pp. 281, 283.

[6] *Ibid.,* pp. 255-56.

[7] It could therefore be observed that, though Jehovah's Witnesses are basically Arian in their view of Christ and the Trinity, they are actually more heretical than the Arians were.

> We believe . . . in one Lord Jesus Christ, the Son of God, be-
> gotten from the Father, only-begotten, that is, from the substance
> of the Father . . . begotten not made, of one substance with the
> Father. . . .[8]

Specifically directed against the Arians was the closing statement:

> But as for those who say, There was when He was not, and,
> Before being born He was not, and that He came into existence
> out of nothing, or who assert that the Son of God is from a dif-
> ferent . . . substance, or is created, or is subject to alteration or
> change — these the Catholic [that is, universal] Church anathe-
> matizes.[9]

By assuming once again the Arian position on the person of
Christ, Jehovah's Witnesses have separated themselves from historic Christianity. Since the Watchtower Christology is essentially Arian, it may be noted that one finds in the writings of Athanasius (295-373 A.D.), the arch-enemy of Arianism, an effective
refutation of the teachings of the Witnesses about the person
of Christ.[10] Note, for example, the following statement: "Those
who call these men [the Arians] Christians are in great and grievous
error, as neither having studied Scripture, nor understanding
Christianity at all, and the faith which it contains."[11] He adds
that to call the Arians Christians is equivalent to calling Caiaphas a
Christian and to reckon Judas as still among the apostles.[12]
Athanasius further comments that, though the Arians use Scriptural language, and frequently quote Scripture, their doctrine is
thoroughly unscriptural[13] — a statement which could with equal
propriety be made about Jehovah's Witnesses today. At another
place he accuses the Arians of harboring the same error as that

---

[8] Kelly, *op. cit.*, p. 232.

[9] *Ibid.*

[10] A number of these works are to be found in Vol. IV of the *Nicene and Post-Nicene Fathers,* Second Series. Among the more important of these are *On the Incarnation of the Word,* and the *Four Discourses Against the Arians,* both of which are contained in Vol. IV. As one reads the latter work, one is struck again and again by the similarities between Arianism and Watchtower teachings.

[11] *Four Discourses Against the Arians* (trans. by Cardinal Newman), Discourse I, Section 1, in *Nicene and Post-Nicene Fathers* (Grand Rapids: Eerdmans, 1953), Second Series, IV, 306.

[12] *Ibid.*, I, 2 (i.e., Discourse I, Section 2).

[13] *Ibid.*, I, 8.

of the Jews who crucified Jesus since the latter also refused to believe that Jesus was truly God, charging Him with blasphemy because He claimed to be equal with God.[14] Arians, Athanasius alleges, are cloaking Judaism with the name of Christianity.[15]

As can be expected, many of the Scripture passages to which the ancient Arians appealed are also adduced by Jehovah's Witnesses today: passages such as Proverbs 8:22, Colossians 1:15, John 14:28, Mark 13:32, and so on. A large part of Discourse I, all of II, and most of III are occupied with the task of refuting the Arian interpretation of these passages. Though present-day Biblical scholars would not agree with all of Athanasius's exegeses, much of what he says in these Discourses is still valuable for us as we encounter Watchtower misinterpretations of these and kindred passages.

Appealing to John 1:3, which tells us that without the Word nothing was made, Athanasius asks, How then did the Word Himself come into being, if He was one of the "things that were made"? If, on the contrary, all things were made through the Word, the Son Himself cannot have been made, cannot be a mere created work.[16] Athanasius reveals the soteriological motive for his opposition to Arius when he says, "For if, being a creature, He [Christ] had become man, man had remained just what he was, not joined to God; for how had a work been joined to the Creator by a work?"[17] To the same effect is the following:

> But this would not have come to pass [the blessings of our future life in glory], had the Word been a creature; for with a creature the devil, himself a creature, would have ever continued the battle, and man, being between the two, had been ever in peril of death, having none in whom and through whom he might be joined to God and delivered from all fear.[18]

Athanasius's point here is well taken: If Christ was only a creature, as the Arians asserted, what guarantee have we that He really conquered the devil, who is also a creature, and that He truly united us to God? How can a mere creature deliver us from the power of another creature? The same devastating criticism can be leveled against the Christology of the Watchtower.

[14] *Ibid.,* III, 27.
[15] *Ibid.,* III, 28.
[16] *Ibid.,* II, 71.
[17] *Ibid.,* II, 67.
[18] *Ibid.,* II, 70.

CRITIQUE OF WATCHTOWER EXEGESIS

We proceed next to examine some of the more important Watchtower interpretations of Scripture passages bearing on the person of Christ. It will be remembered that the Witnesses claim to be guided only by the Word of God and not at all by the opinions of men. Let us see whether their use of Scripture in connection with the alleged creatureliness of Christ supports their claim.[19]

Old Testament Passages. Beginning with Old Testament passages, let us look first at a text to which Jehovah's Witnesses appeal as teaching that Christ was a created being, Proverbs 8:22. In *What Has Religion Done for Mankind?* this passage is quoted in Moffatt's translation, "The Eternal formed me first of his creation, first of all his works in days of old"; previous to this quotation the comment is made: "In the proverbs of wisdom he [Jehovah's only-begotten son] speaks of himself as wisdom and calls attention to his being a creation of the eternal heavenly Father."[20]

It is interesting to observe that the ancient Arians also used this passage to support their views of the person of Christ, utilizing the Septuagint translation of the verse, "The Lord created me (*ektise*) . . . ."[21] So much did the Arians make of this text, in fact, that Athanasius felt it necessary to devote the major part of his second Discourse against the Arians to an exposition of this passage.[22]

Though Proverbs 8:22 figured largely in the Christological controversies of the early centuries, most modern interpreters agree that the purpose of the author of Proverbs here was not to give a dogmatic description of the "origin" of the Second Person of the Trinity, but rather to set forth the value of wisdom as a guide to be followed by believers. In pursuit of this purpose, the author presents a poetic personification of wisdom. By this personified wisdom the statement is made, "Jehovah possessed me in the beginning of his way, before his works of old."[23]

---

[19] Needless to say, no attempt will here be made to give an exhaustive survey of the Biblical evidence for the deity of Christ. The material which follows is an endeavor to refute the type of Biblical interpretation the Witnesses adduce to support their view of Christ.

[20] P. 37. Cf. *The Truth Shall Make You Free,* p. 43, where a similar use is made of the passage.

[21] Kelly, *op. cit.,* p. 230.

[22] Discourse II, Sections 18-82.

[23] ASV. A marginal note appended to the word *possessed* reads: "or formed." The Hebrew verb here used, *qanah,* may also be rendered *begat*

The point of the passage is that wisdom is older than creation and therefore deserves to be followed by all. To use Proverbs 8:22 as ground for a denial of the eternity of the Son — a doctrine clearly taught in the rest of Scripture — is to use the passage in an unwarranted manner.[24]

Isaiah 9:6 is commonly understood by Christians to be one of the clearest Old Testament attestations to the deity of Jesus Christ found anywhere. In the *New World Translation* it reads as follows: "For there has been a child born to us, there has been a son given to us; and the princely rule will come to be upon his shoulder. And his name will be called Wonderful Counselor, Mighty God, Eternal Father, Prince of Peace." It is acknowledged even by Jehovah's Witnesses that this passage predicts the coming Messiah. Yet the Witnesses evade the clear teaching of the passage when they say, "He [Jesus Christ] is a 'mighty God,' but not the Almighty God who is Jehovah (Isa. 9:6)."[25] The fact of the matter is, however, that the Hebrew expression here translated *Mighty God* (*'eel gibboor*) is also used in Isaiah 10:21, where the *New World Translation* has: "A mere remnant will return, the remnant of Jacob, to the Mighty God." It becomes clear from verse 20 of this chapter that the "Mighty God" to whom the remnant of Jacob is said to be about to return is none other than Jehovah, the Holy One of Israel. Yet precisely the same Hebrew expression, *'eel gibboor,* is used in Isaiah 10:21 and in Isaiah 9:6. If *'eel gibboor* in 10:21 means Jehovah, by what stretch of the imagination may the same phrase in 9:6 be interpreted to mean someone less than Jehovah?

In this connection it ought also to be observed that the Hebrew word *'eel* in Isaiah usually denotes Jehovah, the only true God; when it does not do so (in 44:10, 15, 17; 45:20; 46:6), it is used to describe an idol made by men's hands. Surely Isaiah did not intend to say that the coming Messiah would be an idol god! It ought also to be noted that the expression *'eel gibboor* is, in Old Testament literature, a traditional designation of Jehovah —

(see C. F. Burney, "Christ as the ARCHEE of Creation," *Journal of Theological Studies,* XXVII [1926], 160-77).

[24] Cf. Franz Delitzsch, *Commentary on Proverbs, ad loc.;* W. H. Gispen, *De Spreuken Van Salomo* (Kampen: Kok, 1952), pp. 133-34; and Kenneth S. Kantzer, "Wisdom," in Baker's *Dictionary of Theology* (Grand Rapids: Baker, 1960), p. 554.

[25] *The Truth Shall Make You Free,* p. 47.

see Deuteronomy 10:17, Jeremiah 32:18, and Nehemiah 9:32.[26]
We are forced to conclude that Jehovah's Witnesses have not listened to Scripture here, but have simply imposed their preconceived view of Christ upon the Bible.

New Testament Passages. Probably the best-known New Testament passage to which the Witnesses appeal is John 1:1, which
is translated in the 1961 edition of the *New World Translation*
as follows: "In [the] beginning the Word was, and the Word was
with God, and the Word was a god." Note that the word *God*
is capitalized the first time it occurs in the text but not the second
time, and that in the second instance it is preceded by the indefinite
article. The impression this translation intends to convey is that
the Word (Jesus Christ) is not God but *a god* — not equal to
Jehovah God but a subordinate deity.

By way of refutation, it should be observed, first, that Jehovah's
Witnesses thus take a polytheistic position, affirming that there
exists, besides Jehovah God, someone who is a lesser god. This
position is, however, in direct conflict with Scripture, which affirms
in Deuteronomy 4:35, "You have been shown, so as to know that
Jehovah is the [true] God; there is no other besides him" (NWT);
and in I Corinthians 8:4, "We know that an idol is nothing in
the world, and that there is no God but one" (NWT). How,
then, can the Witnesses affirm that Jesus Christ is *a god?* To be
sure, the New Testament does occasionally speak of gods other
than Jehovah, but then only in the sense of false gods. So, for
example, in Acts 28:6 the term *a god* (*theon*) describes what the
superstitious inhabitants of Malta thought Paul was after they
had observed that the viper did not harm him.[27] And in
Galatians 4:8 Paul observes, "Nevertheless, when you did not know
God, then it was that you slaved for those who by nature are not
gods (*theois*)" (NWT). Do the Watchtower theologians intend
to teach that Jesus Christ is a god in one of the two senses just
described? Yet the only times the New Testament speaks of
gods (*theoi*) other than Jehovah is when it is describing false gods

[26] The only difference between these expressions and the one in Isa. 9:6
is the addition of the word *gadool* (meaning great), and of the definite article. In Isa. 10:21, however, the definite article is also missing; yet the
reference is unmistakably to Jehovah. Cf. Delitzsch's *Commentary on the
Prophecies of Isaiah* on Isa. 9:6.

[27] Cf. also Acts 14:11, where the multitude at Lystra is reported as saying about Paul and Barnabas, "The gods [*hoi theoi*] have . . . come down
to us" (NWT).

or idols.[28]   By calling Jesus Christ *a god,* therefore, Jehovah's Witnesses are actually making themselves guilty of idolatry and polytheism.

In an appendix found on pages 773-77 of their *New World Translation of the Christian Greek Scriptures* (published in 1951), the Watchtower editors explain why they have rendered John 1:1 as they did.   They make clear that when the word *theos* (the Greek word for God) first appears in this verse, it occurs with a definite article *(pros ton theon)*, whereas when it appears the second time, it does not have the definite article *(kai theos een ho logos)*.   The editors go on to justify their translation, "and the Word was a god," by saying,

> Careful translators recognize that the articular construction of the noun [that is, the construction in which a noun appears with the definite article] points to an identity, a personality, whereas an anarthrous construction [a construction in which a noun appears without a definite article] points to a quality about someone (p. 774).

In refutation, let it be emphatically stated that this observation is simply not true to fact.   In the article on *theos* in the most recent Greek-English Lexicon of the New Testament, it is said that *theos* is used in the New Testament "quite predominantly of the true God, sometimes with, sometimes without the article."[29]   As a matter of fact, Jehovah's Witnesses do not follow the above-mentioned rule themselves in their *New World Translation.*   In the very chapter in which John 1:1 is found, for example, the word *theos* occurs at least four other times without the definite article, and yet in each instance it is rendered *God,* not *a god.* In John 1:6 we read, in the *New World Translation,* "There arose a man that was sent forth as a representative of God; his name was John."   Since the Greek has *para theou* (no definite article), the Witnesses, to be consistent with their observation about the function of the definite article, ought to translate: "sent from *a god."*   Yet here they render the anarthrous *theos* by *God.*   In verse 12 the expression *tekna theou* (again the anarthrous *theos*)

---

[28] It might be objected that in Jn. 10:34 and 35 the term gods (*theoi*) is applied to Old Testament judges.   Yet surely the Witnesses do not intend to say that Christ is a god only in the sense in which these judges could be called gods since they affirm that Christ is superior to all other creatures.

[29] Wm. F. Arndt and F. Wilbur Gingrich, *Greek-English Lexicon of the New Testament* (Chicago: University of Chicago Press, 1957), p. 357.

is rendered "God's children," and in verse 13 the words *ek theou egenneetheesan* are translated "born . . . from God." Why not "children of *a god,"* and "born from *a god"*? In the 18th verse we read: "No man has seen God at any time." But the Greek again has the anarthrous *theos*: *Theon oudeis heeooraken.* Why do the Witnesses not translate, "No man hath seen *a god* at any time"? The above makes clear that Jehovah's Witnesses do not really believe their own statement about the articular and anarthrous construction of the noun since they do not follow this rule in their own translation. We are compelled to conclude that they translate John 1:1 as they do, not on the basis of careful grammatical study of the Bible, but on the basis of their own doctrinal presuppositions.

In the particular construction in which *theos* occurs in the last part of John 1:1, it functions as a predicate noun preceding the copulative verb *een,* meaning *was.* The authors of the appendix alluded to above contend that the absence of the article before the predicate noun in John 1:1 indicates that the predicate noun designates merely the class to which the subject is referred and excludes the idea that the Word is the same God as the God with whom he is said to be (pp. 774-75).

In reply, however, it should be observed that, according to a recognized Greek scholar,

> A definite predicate nominative has the article when it follows the verb; it does not have the article when it precedes the verb. . . . The opening verse of John's Gospel contains one of the many passages where this rule suggests the translation of a predicate as a definite noun. . . . The absence of the article [before *theos*] does *not* make the predicate indefinite or qualitative when it precedes the verb; it is indefinite in this position only when the context demands it. The context makes no such demand in the Gospel of John, for this statement cannot be regarded as strange in the prologue of the gospel which reaches its climax in the confession of Thomas [John 20:28, "My Lord and my God"].[30]

In the light of Colwell's rule, a definite article is not needed before the second *theos* in John 1:1 in order to make it definite. As a matter of fact, the Witnesses themselves testify to the validity of Colwell's rule in their translation of John 19:21, which in the *New World Translation* reads as follows: "However, the chief

[30] Ernest C. Colwell, "A Definite Rule for the Use of the Article in the Greek New Testament," *Journal of Biblical Literature,* LII (1933), 13, 21.

priests of the Jews began to say to Pilate: 'Do not write, "The King of the Jews," but that he said, "I am King of the Jews" '." Though in the earlier part of the verse the word for king has the definite article (*ho basileus*), in the latter part the word occurs without the definite article (*basileus eimi toon Ioudaioon*). The construction here is quite parallel to that in John 1:1, since *basileus* is a predicate noun, preceding the copulative verb *eimi* (I am). In accordance with previous policy, therefore, the Watchtower translators should have rendered these words: "I am *a king* of the Jews." Quite inconsistently, however, they here consider the predicate noun definite, though it lacks the definite article: "I am King of the Jews." Why, then, did they not consider the predicate noun definite in John 1:1?

The answer is not difficult to find. Jehovah's Witnesses themselves tell us why they have adopted their rendering of John 1:1 on page 774 of the afore-mentioned appendix:

> . . . It is presumptuous to say . . . that the sentence should therefore be translated "and the Word was God." That would mean that the Word was the God with whom the Word was said to be. This is unreasonable; for how can the Word be with the God and at the same time be that same God?[31]

It has thus become clear that the ultimate ground for the Witnesses' translation of this important passage is not the authority of Scripture, but their own rationalistic, anti-Trinitarian theology. What they are saying, in effect, is this: we refuse to accept as Scriptural what our minds cannot grasp!

At this time the reader's attention is called to what is perhaps the most scholarly refutation of Watchtower teachings on the person of Christ ever penned: *The Jehovah's Witnesses and Jesus Christ,* by Bruce M. Metzger, Professor of New Testament Language and Literature at Princeton Theological Seminary.[32] In this twenty-page article Professor Metzger adduces several Scripture passages which prove the full deity of Jesus Christ and then proceeds to attack the Jehovah-Witness translations and exegeses

---

[31] Trinitarians would reply that, though the relationship between the Father and the Son is not rationally explicable, it is nevertheless not contrary to reason. If the Triune God consists of three Persons in one Being, the Son can be both with God and God.

[32] Originally published in the April, 1953, issue of *Theology Today*, this article has been reprinted in pamphlet form and may be obtained from the Theological Book Agency, Princeton, N. J., at 15 cents per copy, or eight copies for one dollar.

of a number of New Testament passages dealing with the person of Christ. Anyone desiring a competent evaluation of Watchtower exegetical methods should obtain a copy of Metzger's article.

Professor Metzger shows, for example, on pages 76-77 of this article that the Witnesses have without any warrant whatever inserted the word *other* four times into their translation of Colossians 1:15-17. The latter part of the 16th verse, for example, which in the American Standard Version reads as follows, "all things have been created through him, and unto him," has been translated by Jehovah's Witnesses as follows: "All other things have been created through him and for him." Since the word *other* is not found in the Greek text in any one of these places, Metzger concludes that the word has simply been inserted by the translators "in order to make the passage refer to Jesus as being on a par with other created things." We see again that the Witnesses have smuggled their own theology into their translations.[33]

On page 78 one will find a discussion of the Watchtower translation of Philippians 2:6, "Who [Christ], although he was existing in God's form, gave no consideration to a seizure, namely, that he should be equal to God." The impression given by this translation is that Christ was not equal to God and even scorned such an equality. Metzger proceeds to show that this translation rests upon a misunderstanding of the Greek.

Next Dr. Metzger indicates that the *New World Translation* obscures the clear attestation of two New Testament passages to the deity of Christ: Titus 2:13 and II Peter 1:1 (p. 79). He cites Granville Sharp's rule, that when a Greek *kai* (and) "connects two nouns of the same case, if the article precedes the first noun and is not repeated before the second noun, the latter always refers to the same person that is expressed or described by the first noun." On the basis of this principle of Greek grammar, Metzger contends that Titus 2:13 should be translated, "the

---

[33] Whereas in the 1951 ed. of the *New World Translation of the Christian Greek Scriptures* the word *other* was simply inserted into the text without any punctuation marks, in the revised ed. of 1961 brackets have been placed around the word *other* in these four instances. On p. 6 of the latter ed. we read, "Brackets enclose words inserted to complete or clarify the sense in the English text." Though the addition of brackets makes it clear that the word *other* is not found in the original, the retention of the word in the revised edition indicates that the interpretation underlying this mistranslation has not been repudiated.

appearing of the glory of our great God and Saviour Jesus Christ";
and that II Peter 1:1 should be rendered, "the righteousness of
our God and Saviour Jesus Christ."[34]

On pages 79-80 Metzger criticizes the *New World* rendering of
Revelation 3:14, which makes the exalted Christ refer to himself as "the beginning of the creation by God." He points out
that "by God" would have required the preposition *hupo,* whereas
the Greek has the genitive case, *tou Theou,* which means *of God*
and not *by God.* The passage, Metzger concludes, does not teach
that Christ was created by God but rather that He is the origin
or primary source of God's creation.

On pages 81-82 Metzger takes up passages which seem to
teach a subordination of the person of the Son to the Father.
He makes clear, for example, that John 14:28, "My Father is
greater than I," does not intend to picture a permanent subordination of the Son to the Father, but rather describes Christ's
condition while in the state of humiliation in contrast to the
celestial glory which He was about to receive.

Christ as the Son of God. The most recent Jehovah-Witness
publication in which their view of the person of Christ is set
forth and defended is a 64-page booklet published in 1962,
entitled *"The Word" — Who Is He? According to John.* Though
much that is found in this booklet simply repeats what had been
taught in earlier publications, one or two points made here will
require some attention. The authors claim that the title *Son
of God,* ascribed to Christ by John the Baptist, Nathanael, John
the apostle, Martha, and the Jews, implied that Christ was not
the Second Person of the Trinity but a person inferior to God the
Father (pp. 19-20; 24ff.). In proof of this contention the
authors adduce Christ's discussion with the Jews who had taken
up stones to stone him, recorded in John 10. Though Jesus
here said, "I and the Father are one," the authors contend, he
did not claim to be equal to the Father, but rather claimed to be
less than God (pp. 25-26). Though the Old Testament spoke of
certain judges as "gods" (verse 35 of John 10, referring to Ps.
82:6), Jesus, it is said, here only claimed to be the *Son* of God;
hence the Jews were quite in error when they thought Christ was
uttering blasphemy (pp. 27-28).

---

[34] It is significant to note that at both of these places the RSV, which
some years ago was accused by certain conservative theologians of having
liberal leanings, gives a clearer testimony to the deity of Christ than either
the KJ or the ASV!

By way of refutation, it should first be pointed out that, according to John 5:18, the Jews sought to kill Jesus "because not only was he breaking the Sabbath but he was also calling God his own Father, making himself equal to God" (NWT). The Jews, therefore, did not understand the expression *Son of God* as Jehovah's Witnesses apparently do. For the latter, the term means someone inferior to the Father. By the Jews of Jesus' day, however, the term was interpreted as meaning full equality with the Father, and it was on account of this claim that they sought to kill him.[35]

This point becomes quite clear when we compare John 10:33 with 10:36. The former verse reads, "We [the Jews] are stoning you [Jesus], not for a fine work, but for blasphemy, even because you, although being a man, make yourself a god" (NWT).[36] The latter passage reads, "Do you say to me whom the Father sanctified and dispatched into the world, 'You blaspheme,' because I said, I am God's Son?" (NWT). Putting together these two verses (if we translate verse 33 as in the standard versions), we see that Christ's calling himself the Son of God was interpreted by the Jews as a claim to equality with the Father.

When Jesus was tried by Caiaphas, furthermore, He was asked, "By the living God I put you under oath to tell us whether you are the Christ the Son of God!" (Mt. 26:63, NWT). After Jesus had answered this question in the affirmative, the high priest is reported to have said, "He has blasphemed! What further need do we have of witnesses?" (v. 65, NWT). Obviously, the high priest understood the expression *Son of God* as meaning full equality with the Father since he called Jesus' assumption of this title blasphemy. If Jesus meant by the term *Son of God* something less than equality with the Father, He would by His affirmative answer be guilty of uttering an untruth, since for the

---

[35] According to Lev. 24:16 one who blasphemed the name of Jehovah was to be put to death by stoning. Since, in the eyes of these Jews, Jesus was a mere man, his claim to equality with the Father was considered blasphemy by them — a sin worthy of the death penalty.

[36] Here the NWT is quite misleading. In the light of John 5:18, quoted above, what the Jews accused Jesus of was the claim of being equal to Jehovah God. Though the definite article is missing before *theon* in 10:33 (it occurs only in p[66], *prima manus*), it is found in 5:18, where the reason why the Jews sought to kill Jesus is also stated: he made himself equal to God (*too theoo*). 10:33 should therefore be rendered as in the KJ, ASV, and RSV: "make yourself God."

Sanhedrin this title meant such equality. Surely if Jesus did not intend His words to be understood as meaning what the high priest and the rest of the Sanhedrin thought they meant, He could have and should have corrected their understanding of these words.

When, after the trial before Caiaphas, Jesus appeared before Pilate, the Jews said to the governor, "We have a law, and according to the law he [Jesus] ought to die, because he made himself God's son" (Jn. 19:7, NWT).[37]   Again it is crystal-clear that the Jews understood the expression *Son of God,* which Jesus acknowledged as descriptive of himself, as meaning nothing less than full equality with the Father. Is it likely, now, that present-day Jehovah's Witnesses know better what Jesus claimed to be, when He called Himself the Son of God, than the Jews who were His contemporaries?

Christ as the Proper Object of Worship.   What do Jehovah's Witnesses do with what is perhaps the clearest direct affirmation of the deity of Christ in the New Testament, the words of Thomas to the risen Jesus, "My Lord and my God"?   Four pages of *"The Word" — Who is He? According to John* are devoted to an exposition of this passage (pp. 48-51).   Before evaluating the interpretation of this text found in this booklet, however, we must first observe what the rest of the New Testament teaches about Christ as a proper object of worship.

The Greek word *proskuneoo,* usually translated worship, is used some sixty times in the New Testament. It may occasionally designate the deference given by one man to another who is his superior, as in Matthew 18:26, where the RSV translates "imploring him."   The word is used in Revelation 3:9 to describe the honor which will be rendered to the church at Philadelphia by those who were of the synagogue of Satan.[38]

The word *proskuneoo* is, however, much more frequently used to describe the worship of God. It is so used in the following passages: Matthew 4:10, Luke 4:8, John 4:21-24, I Corinthians 14:25, Revelation 4:10, 7:11, 14:7, 19:4, 10, 22:9.   Christ Himself, in fact, affirms with unmistakable clarity that worship in the sense of religious veneration may be offered to God alone.

---

[37] Why in this instance the NWT does not capitalize the word *son,* whereas in Mt. 26:63, giving the high priest's question to Jesus, the word *son* is capitalized, we are not told.

[38] Lenski, however, is of the opinion that *proskuneoo* here designates the worship of the exalted Christ in the presence of the Philadelphian church (*The Interpretation of St. John's Revelation,* p. 143).

For when the devil asks Jesus to fall down and worship him (*proskuneoo*), Jesus replies, "It is Jehovah your God you must worship (*proskuneoo*), and it is to him alone you must render sacred service" (Mt. 4:10, NWT).[39]   On the basis of these words of Jesus, therefore, it should be clear that, if Jesus Christ is not the same being as Jehovah, he may not be worshiped by men.   Jehovah's Witnesses teach that Jesus Christ is not the same being as Jehovah.   We should therefore expect to find the New Testament forbidding the worship of Christ.   On the contrary, however, we find that in the New Testament the worship of Christ is not only permitted but praised.

By way of negation, we should observe that the worship of certain individuals other than Jehovah or Christ is specifically forbidden.   As we just saw, Jesus refused to worship the devil. In the book of Revelation the worship of the beast — an apocalyptic symbol of anti-Christian worldly power — is considered the epitome of rebellion against God, punishable by everlasting torment (Rev. 14:9-11).   In three specific instances in the New Testament, worship is offered to individuals only to be rejected by them.   When Cornelius falls down to worship Peter, the latter declines to be so honored, saying, "I myself am also a man" (Acts 10:25-26, NWT).   When John the Apostle falls down to worship the one who has been speaking to him, the latter says, "Be careful!   Do not do that!   All I am is a fellow slave of you and of your brothers who have the work of witnessing to Jesus.   Worship God" (Rev. 19:10, NWT).[40]   And when John again falls down in worship, this time before the feet of the angel that had been showing him the things he had seen, the angel says, "Be careful!   Do not do that!   All I am is a fellow slave of you and of your brothers who are prophets and of those who are observing the words of this scroll.   Worship God" (Rev. 22:9, NWT).   Note that in the last two passages it is explicitly asserted that John may not worship creatures but may worship only God![41]

[39] Jesus is here quoting Deut. 6:13, where the Hebrew has *Yahweh Elooheykha*, Jehovah your God.   In both the Matthew passage and the parallel passage in Luke (4:8), in fact, Christ is reported as having added a word which does not occur in the Hebrew: the word *alone* (NWT) or *only* (KJ, ASV, & RSV).   Christ thus makes the command even more explicitly exclusive than it is in Deuteronomy.

[40] Some commentators hold that the individual here spoken of is an angel, whereas others suggest that he was a fellow man.   In either interpretation, he was only a creature; hence John was not permitted to worship him.

[41] In each passage alluded to in the above paragraph, the Greek word for worship is *proskuneoo*.

What, now, about Jesus Christ? Is there any indication in the New Testament that Christ prohibited people from worshiping him, as Peter did and as the angel did? Did Christ ever say to anyone: "Do not worship me, for I am only a creature. Worship God but do not worship me"? There is no such indication. On the contrary, we find numerous instances where people do worship Christ; in some of these the worship is commended or recognized as evidence of true faith, and in none of these is this worship forbidden.

Let us look at some of these instances. The leper described in Matthew 8:2 worshiped Jesus (ASV).[42] A ruler, identified by the other Synoptists as Jairus, is reported as worshiping Jesus (Matt. 9:18, ASV). After Jesus had walked on the water and had quieted the wind, the disciples are said to have worshiped him, saying, "Of a truth thou art the Son of God" (Mt. 14:33, ASV).[43] The Canaanitish woman worshiped Jesus, saying, "Lord, help me" (Mt. 15:25, ASV). The man born blind, having been informed by Jesus that He was the Son of man, said, "Lord, I believe. And he worshiped him" (Jn. 9:35, 38, ASV).[44]

[42] The NWT here renders the verb *proskuneoo* as *doing obeisance*, though in many of the passages previously discussed it rendered this verb with the word *worship*. On p. 9 of the 1951 ed. of the *New World Translation of the Christian Greek Scriptures*, it is said, "To each major word [of the New Testament] we have assigned one meaning and have held to that meaning as far as the context permitted." In the case of the word *proskuneoo*, however, the translators of the NWT have not assigned the same meaning throughout; sometimes they render this word *worship*, and sometimes *do obeisance*. It will be granted, of course, that there are instances in the New Testament where *proskuneoo* does not mean worship in the full sense of the word (e.g., in Mt. 18:26, in Mk. 15:19, and probably in Rev. 3:9). But the question is whether Jehovah's Witnesses are warranted in using the weaker expression, *do obeisance*, in every instance where *proskuneoo* is used in connection with Jesus (except in Heb. 1:6, where even the NWT has *worship*). One suspects that it is not grammatical but theological considerations which have led them to translate the verb in this way.

[43] Though the NWT again has *did obeisance* rather than *worship*, it is quite clear that the honor shown to Christ by the disciples at this time was not mere deference to a superior creature, but the worship of one recognized as equal to God. Earlier Matthew had recorded the words of the Father at Jesus' baptism: "This is my beloved Son, in whom I am well pleased" (3:17). In the light of these earlier words, in the light of Jewish monotheism, and in the light of what was said about the Jewish understanding of the expression *Son of God*, surely nothing less could have been meant here than the worship of Christ as one who was God!

[44] Though the ASV text here has *Son of God*, *Son of man* is found in the older mss., and is therefore the better reading. It is quite evident from the context, however, that what is denoted here by *proskuneoo* is not mere respect for a person in authority, but religious worship — worship which is, in fact, an act of faith.

After Jesus' resurrection, the women who ran from the empty tomb and the disciples on the mountain in Galilee are said to have worshiped Him (Mt. 28:9 and 17, ASV). In each of the above instances the same word is used which is used of the worship of God: *proskuneoo*. In each of the above instances Jesus willingly receives the worship rendered to Him, and in no case does He tell anyone not to worship Him. And yet this is the same Jesus who had said to Satan, "Thou shalt worship (*proskuneoo*) the Lord thy God, and him only shalt thou serve" (Mt. 4:10, ASV). And the same New Testament which clearly forbids the worship of a creature — even of an angelic creature — both permits and approves the worship of Jesus Christ. Surely here is clear proof of Christ's deity!

To all of this Jehovah's Witnesses might reply: the obeisance which was shown to Jesus by these various individuals was only a kind of respect shown to a superior creature, and does not imply that Jesus was God. How shall we answer this objection?

It will be granted that the word *proskuneoo* when used by New Testament writers does not always designate the adoration of God. As we have seen, it may occasionally be used of an act of respect paid to a creature. But it is clear from Jesus' own words, as recorded in Matthew 4:10, that when *proskuneoo* designates an act of religious veneration, it means *worship,* and that such worship as is described by this word may be offered *only to God.* And it will also be clear to anyone who takes the trouble to study the instances just enumerated that the act described in these passages by *proskuneoo* was nothing less than religious veneration.[45]

It should further be noted that, according to Watchtower teaching, Jesus Christ while on earth was only a man, the exact equivalent of Adam before the fall.[46] When Peter told Cornelius not to worship him (Acts 10:25-26), the former gave as his reason for refusing this worship: "I myself am also a man"

---

[45] Though this is not specifically stated in the instances of the leper and of Jairus, it will be remembered that both of these men prostrated themselves before Jesus because they believed that He could perform a miracle for them. Though this act may not yet have been an expression of true, saving faith at that moment, it was certainly an act of religious veneration in each case. One might counter by saying that the apostles, who were only human, also performed miracles. True, but people did not prostrate themselves before the apostles in worship. When one person began to do so, he was rebuked (Acts 10:25-26).

[46] See above, pp. 63-64, 66.

(NWT). Here the *New World Translation* renders *proskuneoo* with *did obeisance*. If, now, Peter had to tell someone not to do obeisance to him because he was only a man, by what right could Jesus Christ, who according to Watchtower teachings was only a man, receive obeisance from people without rebuking them?

After Jesus' resurrection, so the Witnesses teach, he became a spirit-creature, higher in status than he had been when he lived on earth as a man, but still only a creature. The life he now enjoys is not the life of a divine Person with a human nature but the life of an exalted angel called Michael.[47] In Revelation 22:9, however, the angel who had been speaking to John told the latter not to fall down and worship him (*proskuneoo*), but to worship (*proskuneoo*) only God. If Christ after his resurrection was only an angel — higher, to be sure, than the other angels, but less than God — how could he accept the worship (*proskuneoo*) of the women and the disciples without rebuking them?

All these instances in which Jesus was worshiped come to a climax in the adoration of Thomas recorded in John 20:28. When Thomas saw Jesus the week after he had expressed disbelief in Jesus' resurrection, he said to Him, "My Lord and my God!" (NWT). If Jesus were not God, he should have rebuked Thomas at this point. Instead of rebuking him, however, Jesus praised Thomas, saying, "Because you have seen me have you believed? Happy are those who do not see and yet believe" (v. 29, NWT). Surely here is indisputable proof that Jesus recognized Himself to be God and not only permitted but encouraged believers to worship Him as such!

What, now, do Jehovah's Witnesses do with this verse? On one occasion a Witness who came to the author's door affirmed that when Thomas said, "My Lord," he was looking at Jesus, but that when he said, "My God," he was looking up to heaven and addressing the Father. As Professor Metzger has pointed out, however, the introductory words make this interpretation impossible: "Thomas said to him [that is, to Jesus]: 'My Lord and my God!' " (NWT).[48]

In *"The Word" — Who is He? According to John* the Witnesses now grant that Thomas did say all of these words to Jesus. They go on to assert, however, that if Thomas had meant that Jesus was the only true God, Jesus would certainly have reproved him. Since

---

[47] See above, pp. 65-67.
[48] *Op. cit.*, p. 71, n. 13.

Jesus did not reprove him, so they argue, Thomas could not have meant this (p. 50). What, then, did Thomas mean when he said to Jesus, "My God"? He meant what the Apostle John meant: that Jesus was the Son of God (20:31). John did not say that Jesus was *God the Son;* he only said that Jesus was the *Son of God.* By *Son of God* John meant a being who was not the Second Person of the Trinity but a created being inferior to the Father (pp. 50-51).[49]

This interpretation, however, is a bold attempt to evade the clear teaching of the passage. In refutation of the Jehovah-Witness exegesis of John 20:28, I offer the following considerations:

(1) What can the expression "my God" possibly mean other than "my true God"? As we saw above, the New Testament recognizes no true God beside Jehovah God; any god other than Jehovah is for New Testament writers a false god or an idol. Thomas, being a Jew, was a strict monotheist; for him there was no God beside Jehovah. When he said, "my God," he could have meant nothing other than "my one and only true God."[50]

(2) The argument the Witnesses use to bolster their interpretation boomerangs against them. Here was a monotheistic Jew saying to Jesus: "My God!" The fact that Jesus did not rebuke Thomas but commended him for his faith proves decisively that Jesus was equal to the Father, that He was Himself very God! When thus understood, Jesus' willingness to be called God by Thomas is quite in harmony with the testimony of the rest of the Bible about Him, and with His willingness to permit men to worship Him.

(3) That the Jehovah-Witness understanding of the expression *Son of God* is erroneous, and that *Son of God* in John's Gospel can mean nothing less than full equality with the Father, has already been shown. There is therefore no contradiction whatever be-

[49] The same general interpretation of this passage, though in greatly condensed form, is found in *The Truth Shall Make You Free*, p. 266.
[50] Though it is true that the definite article is found with *theos* in the Greek of this passage (*ho theos mou*, the god of me), we cannot attach decisive significance to its occurrence here, since the nominative used as a vocative very often takes the definite article as a Semitic idiom (C. F. D. Moule, *An Idiom-Book of New Testament Greek*, pp. 116-117; cf. F. Blass and A. Debrunner, *A Greek Grammar of the New Testament*, trans. R. W. Funk, Sec. 147, (3)). A. T. Robertson (*A Grammar of the Greek New Testament in the Light of Historical Research*, p. 465) makes the same admission. Yet the latter also says, on p. 462, "When Thomas said, '*Ho kurios mou kai ho theos mou*' (Jn. 20:28), he gave Christ full acceptance of his deity and of the fact of his resurrection."

tween Thomas' ascription of full deity to Jesus and John's statement, "These [things] have been written down that you may
believe that Jesus is the Christ the Son of God. . ." (20:31, NWT).

The Jehovah-Witness denial of the deity of Christ must therefore be rejected by all true believers as a heresy which cuts the
very heart out of the Bible. Athanasius put it well: "Jesus whom
I know as my Redeemer cannot be less than God!"

Bibliography

PRIMARY SOURCES:

Russell, Charles T. *Studies in the Scriptures.* 7 Vols. Brooklyn: Watchtower Bible and Tract Soc., 1886-1917.

Rutherford, Joseph F. The following are his major books:
Children (1941).
Creation (1927).
Deliverance (1926).
Enemies (1937)
Government (1928)
The Harp of God (1921). A doctrinal summary.
Jehovah (1934).
Life (1929).
Light (2 vols.; 1930).
Preparation (1933).
Preservation (1932).
Prophecy (1929).
Reconciliation (1928).
Religion (1940).
Riches (1936).
Salvation (1939).
Vindication (3 vols.; 1931 and 1932).

Note: Though Russell's and Rutherford's publications are referred to in *Jehovah's Witnesses in the Divine Purpose,* the authoritative doctrinal guides for the movement today are the volumes which follow. These books, published by the Watchtower Bible and Tract Society since Rutherford's death, have no indication of authorship. They are listed in chronological order.

The New World (1942).
The Truth Shall Make You Free (1943).
The Kingdom is at Hand (1944).
Theocratic Aid to Kingdom Publishers (1945).

Let God Be True (1946; revised in 1952). A summary of the main doctrines taught by Jehovah's Witnesses.
Equipped for Every Good Work (1946). A survey of the contents of the Bible books.
This Means Everlasting Life (1950).
What has Religion Done for Mankind? (1951).
New Heavens and a New Earth (1953).
Make Sure of All Things (1953; revised in 1957). A compilation of Scripture passages on 70 topics.
Qualified to be Ministers (1955; revised and expanded in 1967). How to study the Bible, how to conduct meetings, and how to witness.
You May Survive Armageddon into God's New World (1955).
From Paradise Lost to Paradise Regained (1958).
Your Will be Done on Earth (1958).
Let Your Name Be Sanctified (1961).
All Scripture is Inspired of God and Beneficial (1963).
Babylon the Great Has Fallen! God's Kingdom Rules (1963).
Make Sure of All Things; Hold Fast to What is Fine (1965). A revised and expanded version of *Make Sure of All Things.*
Things in Which it is Impossible for God to Lie (1965).
Life Everlasting — in Freedom of the Sons of God (1966).
Did Man Get Here by Evolution or by Creation? (1967).
Your Word is a Lamp to my Feet (1967).
The Truth that Leads to Eternal Life (1968).
Then is Finished the Mystery of God (1969).
Is the Bible Really the Word of God? (1969).
The Nations Shall Know that I am Jehovah — How? (1971).

The Watchtower Society has published a great number of booklets. Four of the more important titles are listed below:
Defending and Legally Establishing the Good News (1950). This 96-p. booklet, written by Hayden C. Covington, general counsel for Jehovah's Witnesses, gives advice to the Witnesses on legal procedures and lists court decisions upholding their legal rights.
What Do the Scriptures Say about "Survival After Death"? (1955). 96 pp. Discusses the immortality of the soul, and related questions.
Blood, Medicine, and the Law of God (1961). 64 pp. Deals with the question of blood transfusion.
"The Word" — Who Is He? According to John (1962). 64 pp. John's teachings about the Logos.

OFFICIAL GREEK TESTAMENT AND BIBLE TRANSLATIONS:
Wilson, Benjamin. *The Emphatic Diaglott.* Brooklyn: Watchtower

Society, 1942 (first pub. in 1864). An interlinear Greek Testament, based on the recension of J. J. Griesbach (1806).

The New World Translation of the Hebrew Scriptures. Pub. in 5 vols.: Vol. I, Genesis through Ruth (1953); Vol. II, I Samuel through Esther (1955); Vol. III, Job through Song of Solomon (1957); Vol. IV, Isaiah through Lamentations (1958); Vol. V, Ezekiel through Malachi (1960).

The New World Translation of the Christian Greek Scriptures. First pub. in 1950, rev. in 1951.

The New World Translation of the Holy Scriptures. A rev. ed. of the entire translation in one volume, without footnotes. Pub. in 1961. The latest official edition of the *New World Translation.*

HISTORIES OF JEHOVAH'S WITNESSES:

Jehovah's Witnesses in the Divine Purpose. Brooklyn: Watchtower Bible and Tract Society, 1959. This is the official history of the movement.

Qualified to Be Ministers (1955), pp. 297-360, contains a brief history.

Macmillan, A. H. *Faith on the March.* Englewood Cliffs: Prentice-Hall, 1957. A history of the movement told in autobiographical fashion by one of its leaders.

White, Timothy. *A People for His Name.* N. Y.: Vantage Press, 1967. An attempt to write an objective history of the movement, by one who is sympathetic to the Witnesses, though not a Witness himself. Includes the development of doctrine as an integral part of the history.

REFERENCE WORKS:

Aid to Bible Understanding (1971). 1700 pp. People, places, plants, and animals mentioned in the Bible.

Watchtower Publications Index of Subjects Discussed and Scriptures Explained, 1930-1960. Brooklyn, 1961. Indexes subjects treated and Scripture passages commented on in all Watchtower publications for these years, including periodicals.

Yearbook of Jehovah's Witnesses. Published annually. Contains statistics and service reports for the preceding year.

GENERAL WORKS:

BOOKS:

Axup, Edward J. *The Jehovah's Witnesses Unmasked.* New York: Greenwich, 1959.

Cole, Marley. *Jehovah's Witnesses: The New World Society.* New

York: Vantage Press, 1955. A highly sympathetic treatment, acclaimed by Jehovah's Witnesses, but criticized by Martin and Klann, in an appendix to *Jehovah of the Watch Tower,* as not true to fact.

―――. *Triumphant Kingdom.* New York: Criterion Books, 1957.

Czatt, Milton. *The International Bible Students: Jehovah's Witnesses.* New Haven: Yale University Press, 1933. Essay based on a doctoral dissertation.

Dencher, Ted. *The Watchtower Heresy Versus the Bible.* Chicago: Moody Press, 1961. A defense of Christian doctrines against Jehovah-Witness perversions, by a former Witness. Makes much use of Scripture. Includes chapter on methods of approach.

―――. *Why I Left Jehovah's Witnesses.* Fort Washington, Pa.: Christian Literature Crusade, 1966. An account of the author's reasons for leaving the Witnesses, together with a refutation of some Jehovah-Witness doctrines.

Duncan, Homer. *Heart to Heart Talks with Jehovah's Witnesses.* 2nd ed. Lubbock, Texas: Missionary Crusader, n.d. A discussion of a number of Jehovah-Witness doctrines, for the purpose of persuading Witnesses to break with the movement.

Grigg, David H. *Do Jehovah's Witnesses and the Bible Agree?* N. Y.: Vantage Press, 1958. A Biblical refutation of Watchtower doctrines.

Gruss, Edmond C. *Apostles of Denial.* Philadelphia: Presbyterian and Reformed, 1970. 324 pp. A thorough, well-documented examination and exposé of the history, doctrines, and claims of the movement, by a former Jehovah's Witness who is now a professor of history and apologetics. Includes a discussion of Watchtower methods, suggestions for dealing with Jehovah's Witnesses, descriptions of splinter groups, and a personal testimony. The best recent one-volume treatment of the movement.

Haldeman, I. M. *Millennial Dawnism:* The Blasphemous Religion which teaches the Annihilation of Jesus Christ. New York: Chas. Cook, n.d. (before 1914). A refutation of Millennial Dawnism — an early name for Russellism.

Hebert, Gerard, S. J. *Les Temoins de Jehovah.* Montreal: Les Editions Bellarmin, 1960. A critical study by a Jesuit father, treating history and doctrine. Lists every Watchtower publication from Russell's time to the present.

Martin, Walter R., and Klann, Norman H. *Jehovah of the Watch Tower.* Rev. ed. Grand Rapids: Zondervan, 1959. History, methods, and teachings; refutation of major doctrines. One of the more important secondary sources.

McKinney, George D., Jr. *The Theology of the Jehovah's Witnesses.* Grand Rapids: Zondervan, 1962. A systematic exposition of doctrinal teachings. A competent work, though occasionally outdated quotations are used.

Pike, Royston. *Jehovah's Witnesses: Who They Are, What They Teach, What They Do.* New York: Philosophical Library, 1954.

An objective treatment, more complete than most accounts on their eschatology.

Rogerson, Alan. *Millions Now Living Will Never Die.* London: Constable, 1969. An account of the history, beliefs, and organization of the Jehovah-Witness movement by a former Witness. An attempt to give an objective answer to the question, "Who are Jehovah's Witnesses?"

Schnell, Wm. J. *Thirty Years a Watchtower Slave.* Grand Rapids: Baker, 1956. A revealing account of the inner workings of the movement by one who was a Jehovah's Witness for thirty years. Makes a contribution no other book has made.

————. *Into the Light of Christianity.* Grand Rapids: Baker, 1959. Discusses and refutes the main doctrines of Jehovah's Witnesses.

————. *Christians: Awake!* Grand Rapids: Baker, 1962. Deals chiefly with methods of witnessing to Jehovah's Witnesses.

Spier, H. J. *De Jehovah's Getuigen en de Bijbel.* 2nd enlarged ed. Kampen: Kok, 1971. Paperback, 191 pp. A competent analysis and refutation of the main doctrines. Includes a 19-p. glossary of Watchtower terms.

Stevenson, W. C. *The Inside Story of Jehovah's Witnesses.* N. Y.: Hart Publishing Co., 1968 (orig. pub. by Hutchinson of London [1967] under the title, *Year of Doom, 1975*). An evaluation of the movement from the inside, by one who was an active Witness for 14 years. Includes such matters as the appeal of the movement, the inner working of the Watchtower Society, a critical discussion of Watchtower teachings and practices, and suggestions on how to deal with Witnesses. More irenic than Schnell's *Thirty Years a Watchtower Slave.*

Stroup, Herbert H. *The Jehovah's Witnesses.* New York: Columbia Univ. Press, 1945. An objective, scholarly study, based on a doctoral dissertation.

Thomas, F. W. *Masters of Deception.* Grand Rapids: Baker, 1972. A substantial Biblical refutation of the major Watchtower doctrines, by a layman active in evangelism.

Whalen, Wm. J. *Armageddon Around the Corner.* New York: John Day Co., 1962. A Roman Catholic layman writes about the movement, touching on its history, theology, organization, court activities, and schisms.

PAMPHLETS:

(Note: These are inexpensive, and may be ordered in quantities for distribution.)

Burrell, M. C. *Jehovah's Witnesses.* London: Church Book Room Press, 1960. 20 pp. History, methods, and doctrines.

Kneedler, Wm. Harding. *Christian Answers to Jehovah's Witnesses.*

Chicago: Moody Press, 1953. 64 pp. A brief exposition and refutation of the main doctrines.

Martin, Walter R. *Jehovah's Witnesses.* Grand Rapids: Zondervan, 1957. 64 pp. History, doctrines, and practices.

Mayer, F. E. *Jehovah's Witnesses.* St. Louis: Concordia, 1957. Rev. ed. (first pub. in 1942). 61 pp. Mayer was professor of systematic theology at Concordia Seminary. Leans chiefly on Rutherford; no reference to later publications.

Metzger, Bruce M. *The Jehovah's Witnesses and Jesus Christ.* A reprint from *Theology Today,* Vol. X, No. 1 (April, 1953), pp. 65-85; obtainable from the Theological Book Agency, Princeton, N. J. Metzger is professor of New Testament at Princeton Seminary. A scholarly refutation of the Jehovah-Witness view of Jesus Christ.

Strauss, Lehmann. *An Examination of the Doctrine of Jehovah's Witnesses.* New York: Loizeaux Bros., 1955 (first pub. 1942). 47 pp.

Talbot, Louis T. *What's Wrong with Jehovah's Witnesses?* Findlay, Ohio: Dunham Pub. Co. 50 pp.

Tanis, Edward J. *What the Sects Teach.* Grand Rapids: Baker, 1958. 89 pp. A brief critical treatment of Jehovah's Witnesses (and of Christian Science, Seventh-day Adventism, and Spiritism).

Wassink, A. *The Bible and Jehovah's Witnesses.* Faith, Prayer, and Tract League; Grand Rapids, Mich. 49504. 18 pp. Outdated in some respects, but still useful.

(Note: Some of the above pamphlets can be obtained from Religion Analysis Service, 902 Hennepin Ave., Minneapolis 3, Minn.)

PERIODICALS:

Schnell, Wm. J., ed. *The Converted Jehovah's Witness Expositor.* Published every 3 months at 794 Terrace Road, Dunedin, Florida 33528. The only periodical devoted exclusively to the refutation of Jehovah-Witness errors.